ATHLETES ONCE:
100 FAMOUS PEOPLE WHO
WERE ONCE NOTABLE ATHLETES

ATHLETES ONCE:
100 FAMOUS PEOPLE WHO WERE ONCE NOTABLE ATHLETES

BY

E. W. SMITH, JR.

Cortero Publishing
www.CorteroPublishing.com
An Imprint of Fireship Press

ATHLETES ONCE: 100 Famous People Who Were Once Notable Athletes — Copyright © 2009 by E. W. Smith, Jr.

ISBN: 978-1-61179-068-9

BISAC Subject Headings:
     BIO016000   BIOGRAPHY & AUTOBIOGRAPHY / Sports
     BIO005000   BIOGRAPHY & AUTOBIOGRAPHY / Entertainment
                     & Performing Arts
     BIO013000   BIOGRAPHY & AUTOBIOGRAPHY / Rich & Famous

Address all correspondence to:
Fireship Press, LLC
P.O. Box 68412
Tucson, AZ 85737

Or visit our website at:
www.FireshipPress.com

1.0

Dedication

This book is dedicated to
my three wonderful companions
Joan, my soul mate
and
Max and Lady, my faithful Cairn Terriers

CONTENTS
(Some names will appear in more than one category)

Boxing

Crew

Figure Skating

Fencing

Football

Golf

Gymnastics

PREFACE

This book is intended as a reference source for anyone who has an interest in notable people, their accomplishments, and their backgrounds. More specifically, it is a collection of biographical sketches of famous people who participated in sports in their earlier years.

It is quite amazing to see the variety of noted persons who have excelled in sports while growing up, and then excelled again later on in their respective professions. It leads you to wonder if there is a connection. Is it the competitiveness of sports, the drive to succeed, the ability to focus all of one's talents into a winning formula; or is it just plain God given talent in both sports and beyond? Whatever the reason, it makes for interesting reading.

For example:

Did you know that Dwight Eisenhower, a President of the United States, once tackled the legendary Jim Thorpe while playing linebacker for West Point in a 1912 game against Carlyle Institute? Did you know that Tommy Lee Jones, the world acclaimed actor, is one of the all-time great football players for Harvard University as an offensive lineman? Did you know that George S. Patton, the famous World War II general, participated in the 1912 Olympics in Stockholm; or that Ward Bond, the famous character actor, played on the National Championship football team at the University of Southern California in 1927 as an offensive lineman? How about Dean Martin, the smooth and suave singer? Did you know he was a professional boxer, had twelve fights, and "won every one but eleven"?

These are fascinating stories and I hope you will enjoy reading them as much as I enjoyed the writing.

E. W. Smith, Jr.

JOHN WAYNE

John Wayne was born Marion Morrison on May 26, 1907 in Winterset, Iowa. His father was a pharmacist and developed lung problems, so he moved the family to southern California in 1911. Marion had an Airedale dog, which he had named "Duke," and they were always together, so his friends started calling *him* "Duke."

"Duke" was an outstanding football player at Glendale High School and upon graduation he was awarded a football scholarship to the University of Southern California (USC). He enrolled at USC in September of 1925 and made the first team freshman squad where he played guard. He made the varsity football team in his sophomore year in 1926. In November he tore a shoulder muscle while surfing near the Balboa Beach and never played football after that. He did, however, earn a varsity letter that year, but subsequently lost his scholarship and could not afford to attend college on his own.

The coach, Howard Jones, had him contact Tom Mix, the western cowboy who promised that he would get jobs for USC football players after Jones had gotten tickets for Mix at home games. So in 1926 Marion left USC and went to work for William Fox studios as a prop mover. He eventually met John Ford who liked the young man and got him parts in movies. He was on his way to becoming one of the biggest movies stars ever in Hollywood. John Wayne died on June 11, 1979 in Los Angeles at age 72.

WARD BOND

Ward Bond was born Wardell Bond on April 9, 1903 in Benkelman, Nebraska. He spent most of his childhood in Benkelman, but in 1919 the family moved to Denver, Colorado.

He graduated from East Denver High School and later entered the University of Southern California (USC) where he played football with John Wayne. Bond and Wayne became lifelong friends. Ward was a starting lineman on the 1928 USC team that became national champions.

After college Ward entered the acting business under the guidance of John Ford and made his screen debut in 1929. He was frequently typecast as a friendly policeman or as a brutal thug. He had many roles in such noted movies as *The Searchers, Drums Along the Mohawk. The Quiet Man, Fort Apache, It Happened One Night, It's a Wonderful Life, Bringing up Baby, Gone with the Wind, The Maltese Falcon, Sergeant York, They Were Expendable, Joan of Arc*, and *Rio Bravo*. He would later go on to act in nearly hundreds of films and television and was awarded a star on the Hollywood Walk of Fame. He later starred in the popular NBC western television series *Wagon Train* from 1957 until his death. In the final count, he would have over 200 different roles in movies and television.

Ward was inducted into the Western Performers Hall of Fame at the Cowboy Museum in Oklahoma City. Ward Bond died of a heart attack while in Dallas, Texas to attend a football game at the age of 57 on November 5, 1960. His old buddy John Wayne gave the eulogy at his funeral. Ward Bond was honored with a star on the Hollywood Walk of Fame. There is also a Ward Bond Memorial Park in his birthplace of Benkelman, Nebraska.

JOHNNY MACK BROWN

Johnny Mack Brown was born on September 1, 1904 in Dothan, Alabama. He went to the University of Alabama on a football scholarship where he played halfback and had the nickname the "Dothan Antelope." In the 1926 NCAA Division 1-A football championship game, Alabama played in the Rose bowl against the heavily favored Washington Huskies. He earned Most Valuable Player honors after scoring two of his team's three touchdowns in an upset over Washington.

His good looks and powerful physique saw him portrayed on Wheaties cereal boxes and, in 1927, brought an offer for motion picture screen tests that resulted in a long and successful career in Hollywood.

He played silent film star Mary Pickford's love interest in her first talkie, "*Coquette*", for which Pickford won an Oscar. He appeared in minor roles until 1930 when he was cast as the star in a western movie entitled *Billy the Kid*. Also in 1930, Johnny played Joan Crawford's love interest in *Montana Moon*. He went on to make several more top-flight movies including *The Secret Six* with Wallace Beery, Jean Harlow, and Clark Gable. Shortly thereafter he devoted his acting strictly to exclusively low budget westerns, becoming one of the screen's top B-movie cowboy stars, making more than 127 films until he retired in 1953. Later he would play in supporting roles until 1966.

Johnny would eventually make more than 160 films and have a star on the Hollywood Walk of Fame. He is also in the Alabama Sports Hall of Fame. He died of heart failure in 1974 at the age of 70 at Woodland Hills, California. His cremated remains are interred in an outdoor Columbarium in Glendale's Forest Lawn Cemetery.

RANDOLPH SCOTT

Randolph Scott was born as George Randolph Crane on January 23, 1898 in Orange County, Virginia while his parents were on a visit from North Carolina. At an early age he excelled in football, baseball, and other sports.

In 1917 at the age of 19 he joined Army and served in France as an artillery observer. After the war Randolph stayed in France an enrolled in an artillery officers' school and eventually received a commission. He returned to the United States in 1919 and entered Georgia Tech to get a degree and also play football. He made the varsity team but later injured his back and had to quit football.

He dropped out of Georgia Tech and transferred to the University of North Carolina to major in textile engineering and manufacturing. After college he worked as an accountant at the company where his father worked. He became very interested in acting and moved to California in 1929 to give it a try. He met Howard Hughes on a golf course and Howard got him an audition with Cecil B. De Mille. Because of his southern accent he was hired to coach Gary Cooper in the Virginian but he also had a bit part in the movie. This started his film career and he would go on to star in over 100 movies, mostly westerns, and span a career of nearly 33 years.

He retired in 1962 at the age of 64 as a wealthy man after shrewdly investing his money. He was inducted into the Western Performers Hall of Fame at the Cowboy Museum in Oklahoma City and he also has a star of the Hollywood Walk of Fame. Randolph Scott died in Beverly Hills on March 2, 1987 at the age of 89. He is buried in his old hometown of Charlotte, North Carolina.

JOHNNY
WEISSMULLER

Johnny Weissmuller was born Peter Johann Weissmuller on June 2, 1904 in Romania. He and his family migrated to the United States on January 26, 1905 and by 1910 the clan was living in Windber, Pennsylvania.

When Johnny was 9 years old he contracted polio and his doctor recommended that he start swimming to strengthen his body and fight the disease. Later the family moved to Chicago and Johnny's father bought a bar. After awhile the business failed, and Johnny's parents divorced when the father developed a drinking problem. Meanwhile Johnny continued swimming and won a spot on the YMCA swim team. He eventually dropped out of high school and worked a various jobs to make a living. While working at the Illinois Athletic Club as a bellhop he was noticed by the swim coach and started training the young man. In 1921 Johnny won the national championship in the 50-yard and 220-yard distances and in 1922 set the world record in the 100-meter freestyle. In the 1924 Olympics he won 3 gold medals for swimming and a bronze medal as part of the water polo team. In the 1928 Olympics he won two more gold medals.

In 1929 he signed a contract to be a model for BVDs and was soon being featured in movies. In 1932 he signed a 7 year contract with MGM and started in his first Tarzan movie, *Tarzan the Ape Man.* He became an overnight success and that started his tenure as Tarzan, which lasted until 1948 at which time he started making Jungle Jim movies and TV series. Johnny retired from movies in the late 1950s. He died on January 20, 1984 at the age of 79. He has a star on the Hollywood Walk of Fame.

BUSTER CRABBE

Buster Crabbe was born Clarence Linden Crabbe II on February 2, 1908 in Oakland, California to Lucy and Edward Clinton Crabbe. In 1910 the family was living in a boarding house in Oakland and Edward was working as a real estate broker.

Buster was raised in Hawaii and graduated from Punahou School in Honolulu where he was an excellent swimmer. He participated in two Olympic Games. In the Olympic Games of 1928 he won a bronze medal in the 1500 meter freestyle. After high school he enrolled at the University of Southern California (USC) and became the school's first All-America swimmer in 1931. Buster graduated from USC in 1931 and participated in the 1932 Olympics in Los Angeles where he won a gold medal in the 400 meter freestyle.

In 1933 he married his college sweetheart Adah Virginia Held, and gave himself one year to either make it as an actor or start law school at USC. Buster landed the starring role in the 1933 *Tarzan* serial and *Tarzan the Fearless* which was also issued as a full length movie. These successes launched his career in which he would star in over one hundred movies. He starred in the 1934 movie *Search for Beauty* and in

1936 he played the lead role in the *Flash Gordon* serial. He also made western movies and several *Buck Rogers* movies. Later Buster would star in a television series *Captain Gallant of the Foreign Legion* from 1955 to 1957. He would also make many appearances on the small screen in various roles, including Buck Rogers.

Buster Crabbe died on April 23, 1983 at the age of 75 of a heart attack after tripping over a wastebasket in his Scottsdale, Arizona home. He is buried in the Green Acres Memorial Gardens Cemetery in Scottsdale.

SONJA HENIE

Sonja Henie was born in Oslo, Norway on April 8, 1912 to Wilhelm Henie, a prosperous Norwegian furrier, and his wife Selma. Both parents were financially well off because they both had inherited wealth in addition to their business income.

Wilhelm had been a one-time World Cycling Champion and encouraged his children to take up a variety of sports. Sonja initially showed talent at skiing, and then followed her older brother Leif to take up figure skating. As a girl, Sonja was also a nationally-ranked tennis player and skilled swimmer and equestrienne. Sonja won her first major competition, the senior Norwegian championships, at the age of 9. She placed eighth at the 1924 Winter Olympics at the age of eleven. Sonja won the first of an unprecedented ten World Figure Skating Championships in 1927 at the age of fourteen and her first Olympic gold medal the following year. She also won six consecutive European championships. She was a three-time Olympic Champion in 1928, 1932, and 1936. She won more Olympic and World titles than any other ladies figure skater.

After 1936 Sonja took up a career as a professional performer in acting and live shows. After a successful ice show in Los Angeles, Darryl Zanuck signed her to a long term contract at Twentieth Century Fox, which made her one of the highest-paid actresses of the time. Sonja went on to star in many movies and she also produced Hollywood Ice Revue, a touring ice show which made her rich.

Sonja Henie died of leukemia on October 12, 1969 at the age of 57. She is buried in Oslo on the hilltop overlooking the Henie-Onstad Art Centre.

MARK HARMON

Mark Harmon was born on September 2, 1951 as Thomas Mark Harmon in Burbank, California. His father was the famous Tom Harmon, a University of Michigan All-American football player and winner of the Heisman Trophy, while his mother was a movie actress.

Mark grew up in Burbank and enrolled at Los Angeles Pierce College where he played quarterback on the football team. He later transferred to the University of California at Los Angeles (UCLA) where he started at quarterback in 1972 and 1973. In 1972 Mark and UCLA defeated the defending national champions the University of Nebraska, and in 1973 he was given the National Football Foundation award for All-Round Excellence. During his career at UCLA he won 17 games and lost only 5. He graduated with a B. A. degree in Communications cum laude in 1974.

After graduating from UCLA Mark went into acting and spent much of his career portraying law enforcement and medical personnel. Other than athletics/sports appearances, one of his first national TV appearances was with his father Tom Harmon, in a commercial for Kellogg's Product 19 cereal, for which his father was the longtime TV spokesman. Mark had minor roles in various television series including *Adam-12, Emergency, Police Woman, Laverne and Shirley,* etc. His first major starring role was in a soap opera called *Flamingo Road* and after a short run he was offered the starring role in *St. Elsewhere* in 1983. After several miscellaneous roles in television and movies he landed his current starring role as Leroy Gibbs on the hit CBS television series *NCIS*. In 1986 *People* Magazine named him Sexiest Man Alive.

ROBERT STACK

Robert Stack was born on January 13, 1919 in Los Angeles, California. He grew up in Europe and became fluent in Italian and French. He was raised by his mother, Mary Elizabeth, after his parents were divorced when Robert was a year old. His father, James Langford Stack, a wealthy advertising agency owner, died when Robert was nine.

After returning to Los Angeles from Europe, Robert became very active in skeet shooting and polo. At age 16 he was a member of the All-American Skeet Team and set two world records in skeet shooting and won the National Championship.

Robert took drama classes at Bridgewater State College and at age 20 he took a screen test and was put under contract to Universal Studios. His first movie was *First Love* filmed in 1939; he was the first actor to give Deanna Durbin a screen kiss.

He joined the Navy in World War II and became a gunnery instructor. After the war he returned to Hollywood and continued his film career. In 1957 he was nominated for an Academy Award for his role in *Written on the Wind* and eventually starred in more than 40 films. He starred as Eliot

Ness in the television drama *The Untouchables* from 1959 to 1963. He won an Emmy Award for his role as Ness in 1960. Robert also starred in three other drama series in T*he Name of the Game, Most Wanted,* and *Strike Force.* Known for his steadfast, humorless demeanor, he made fun of his own persona in comedies such as *1941, Airplane* and *Caddyshack II.* He began hosting *Unsolved Mysteries* on television from 1987 to 2002.

Robert Stack died of a heart attack on May 14, 2003 at the age of 84 in Beverly Hills, California. He is a member of the National Skeet Shooting Hall of Fame.

ED MARINARO

Ed Marinaro was bon on March 31, 1950 in New York City. He went to high school in Milford, New Jersey and played football for the Milford High School Knights. He was awarded a scholarship to Cornell where he was an outstanding football player. He set 16 NCAA records and was the first running back in history to run for 4,000 yards. He led the nation in rushing in 1970 and 1971. In 1971 he was the runner up to Pat Sullivan for the Heisman Trophy, the highest finish for an Ivy League player since the league deemphasized football in the mid-1950s. Princeton's Dick Kazmaier won the award in 1951 when the Ivy League was still considered a major football conference. Ed won the 1971 Maxwell Award and the UPI College Football Player of the Year as the top player in college football that year. After college he played 6 seasons of professional football with the Minnesota Vikings, New York Jets, and Seattle Seahawks. He played in Super Bowl VIII and Super Bowl IX with the Vikings and scored 13 touchdowns during his professional career. He was inducted into the College Football Hall of Fame in 1991.

After his football career he became an actor and was a cast member on a number of television series including *The Edge of Night, Laverne and Shirley, Hill Street Blues*, and *Sisters*. He also appeared in the 2006 film *Circus Island*. Ed plays the head football coach on Spike TV's comedy, *Blue Mountain State*, which started airing in January 2010.

Ed Marinaro is currently married to fitness expert Tracy York with whom he has a son, Eddie.

ALAN LADD

Alan Walbridge Ladd was bon in Hot Springs, Arkansas to an American father and an English mother on September 3, 1913. His father died when he was four years old and his mother moved the family to Oklahoma City, where she married a housepainter by the name of Jim Beavers. The family then moved again to North Hollywood, California.

Alan grew up in North Hollywood and in high school he became a swimming and diving champion. He soon became fascinated with drama and acting and decided to become an actor.

His early success was in radio, where his deep and rich baritone voice kept him employed on such shows as *Box 13*. He played small parts in several films, the most significant of which was *Citizen Kane*. He first gained some recognition with a featured role in the wartime thriller *Joan of Paris* in 1942. That same year Alan married his agent/manager Sue Carol, who found him a role in a movie entitled *This Gun for Hire* which was a sensation at the box office. He went on to become one of Paramount Pictures most popular stars. Alan starred in many, many movies of which he most notable was *Shane* in 1953.

Alan Ladd became a wealthy man because of wise business developments with properties in Beverly Hills and Palm Springs. He had three children: Alan Ladd, Jr., daughter Alana, and son David Ladd, who was married to Cheryl Ladd of *Charlie's Angels* fame.

Alan Ladd died in Palm Springs of an acute overdose of alcohol and sedatives at the age of 50. He is buried in the Forest Lawn Cemetery in Glendale, California. He has a star of the Hollywood Walk of Fame and his handprint appears in the forecourt of Grauman's Chinese Theater in Hollywood.

JOE KENNEDY, JR

Joseph Patrick "Joe" Kennedy, Jr., the elder brother of John F., Robert, and Ted Kennedy, was born on July 25, 1915 at Hull, Massachusetts. He was the son of Joseph Patrick Kennedy, Sr. and Rose Elizabeth Kennedy. He attended the Dexter School in Brookline and graduated in 1933.

Joe then entered Harvard University, where he played football, rugby, and crew. He graduated in 1938 and later enrolled in the Harvard Law School. During World War II, Joe left before his final year of law school to begin officer and flight training in the Navy. He earned his wings as a Naval Aviator in May 1942 and was sent to Britain in September 1943 where he piloted land-based PB4Y Liberator patrol bombers on anti-submarine missions in 1943-1944. He had completed 25 combat missions and was eligible to return home; however, he instead volunteered for an Operation Aphrodite mission, which was a series of bombing runs by explosive-laden aircraft piloted by a skeleton crew who would parachute from the aircraft before detonation.

After the plans were drawn, Joe and Lieutenant Wilford John Willy were designated as the first Navy flight crew. They flew a modified version of the B-24 Liberator for the first mission, loaded with 21,170 pounds of Torpex (dynamite). They took off on August 12, 1944. Following in a de Havilland Mosquito to film the mission was Colonel Elliott Roosevelt, son of the President. Ten minutes before the crew was to bail out, the Torpex exploded, killing Joe and Wilford. Joe's body was never recovered and he was posthumously awarded the Navy Cross, the Distinguished Flying Cross and the Air Medal.

ROBERT F. KENNEDY

Robert Francis "Bobby" Kennedy was born on November 20, 1925 in Brookline, Massachusetts. He was the seventh child of Joseph P. and Rose Kennedy and the younger brother of Joe and John F. The family moved around quite a lot and Bobby spent time in Riverdale and Bronxville, New York as a child. He would spend his summers in Hyannis Port, Massachusetts and his Christmas and Easter breaks in their winter home in Palm Springs, Florida. He attended Benedictine boarding school in Milton, Massachusetts for the eighth through the tenth grade. He spent his junior and senior high school years at the Milton Academy, another boarding school in Milton.

After graduation in October, 1943 he enlisted in the Naval Reserve as an apprentice seaman. In March 1944 he transferred to the V-12 College Training Program at Harvard. On December 15 the Navy commissioned the destroyer Joseph P. Kennedy, Jr. and Bobby requested duty on the initial cruise. He was honorably discharged from the Navy on May 30, 1946.

Robert enrolled at Harvard in September, 1946 as a junior being given credit for the V-12 college training. He made the varsity football team as an end and starter. He scored the first touchdown of his senior year before breaking his leg. He graduated in March, 1948 with a B.A. degree in Government. In September 1948 he enrolled at the University of Virginia Law School and graduated in June 1951. He was appointed Attorney General of the United States by his brother John in 1960. After JFK's death in 1963 he won a New York Senate seat and then ran for President in 1968. He was assassinated at the Ambassador Hotel on June 5, 1968. He was buried near his brother in Arlington National Cemetery.

TED KENNEDY

Edward Moore "Ted" Kennedy was born on February 22, 1932 in St. Margaret's Hospital in Boston Massachusetts, the youngest of nine children of Joseph P. Kennedy and Rose Fitzgerald, who were members of prominent Irish-American families and who were amongst the wealthiest families in the nation. Uprooted often as a child, he lived in Bronxville, New York, Hyannis Port, Massachusetts, Palm Beach, Florida, and the Court of St. James's in London. Between the ages of eight and sixteen he suffered the trauma of his sister Rosemary's lobotomy and the deaths of his older brother Joe in World War II and his sister Kathleen in an airplane crash.

Ted went to high school at Milton Academy prep where he played football, tennis, hockey, and was in the drama, debate, and glee clubs. Ted graduated from high school in 1950 and entered Harvard and was assigned to the athlete-oriented Winthrop House, where his brothers had lived. He played as a large, fearless offensive and defensive end of the football team.

Ted was expelled from Harvard for cheating on an exam so he enlisted in the Army in June 1951. His father's political connections ensured he was not deployed to the Korean War.

He re-entered Harvard in 1953 and was a member of the football team until his graduation in 1956. He received a recruiting letter from the Green Bay Packers but rejected the offer saying he was going into politics.

Ted graduated from the University of Virginia Law School in 1959. He was elected to fill his brother John's senate set in 1962. He served outstandingly in the senate until his death from brain cancer on August 25, 2009. He is buried not far from his brothers in Arlington National Cemetery.

DWIGHT DAVID EISENHOWER

Dwight David Eisenhower was born on October 14, 1890 in Denison, Texas, the third of seven boys born to David Jacob Eisenhower and Ida Elizabeth Stover of German, English and Swiss ancestry. The family moved to Abilene, Kansas where he grew up. His father, David Eisenhower, was a college-educated engineer but had trouble making a living; the family was poor. Dwight graduated from Abilene High School in 1909, and Kansas Senator Joseph L. Bristow recommended him for an appointment to West Point in 1911. He had always been called Dwight, so he reversed the order of his names when he entered West Point.

At the Point he was a starter running back for the football team and also played line-backer. In 1912 he once played a game where he tackled the legendary Jim Thorpe. He also played other sports, including basketball and boxing. He graduated in the class of 1915, called "the class the stars fell on," because of the high level of officers it produced.

Dwight married Mamie Doud Eisenhower of Boone, Iowa on July 1, 1916. The couple had two sons, Doud Dwight and Sheldon Doud. Doud Dwight died of scarlet fever in 1921. Dwight went on to an outstanding military career and was the Allied Supreme Commander in Europe in World War II. He was later elected the 34th President of the United States in 1952 and served until 1961.

Eisenhower was an avid golfer and played every chance he got. His favorite course was Augusta National, where he was a member. Dwight or "Ike" died of congestive heart failure at Walter Reed Army Hospital on March 28, 1969. He is buried at the Eisenhower Presidential Library in Abilene, Kansas along with his son Doud Dwight and his wife Mamie.

WILLIAM HALSEY

William Frederick Halsey, Jr., "Bull", was born on October 30, 1882 in Elizabeth, New Jersey, the son of Captain William F. Halsey, Sr., USN. He was a descendent of Senator Rufus King, who was a delegate for Massachusetts to the Continental Congress and attended the Constitutional Convention, and was one of the signers of the United States Constitution on September 17, 1787.

William grew up in Elizabeth, and after graduating from high school he waited around for an appointment to the U. S. Naval Academy. After waiting two years he decided to enroll at the University of Virginia and become a doctor; however, shortly after enrolling he received his appointment to the Naval Academy.

William participated in many sports and was an outstanding football player. He also won several athletic awards while at the Academy. He graduated in 1904 and spent his early service years in battleships and torpedo boats.

Lieutenant Commander Halsey's World War I service, including command of the *USS Shaw* in 1918, was sufficiently distinguished to earn him a Navy Cross. From 1922 through 1925 Halsey served as Naval Attache in Berlin, Germany, and commanded the *USS Dale*. During 1930 – 1932 Captain Halsey led two destroyer squadrons, then studied at the Naval War College in the mid-1930s. Prior to assuming command of an aircraft carrier, he undertook aviator instruction and was awarded his wings. During World War II he was made appointed Fleet Admiral and played a prominent role in the Pacific war. He retired from the Navy in October 1945.

Admiral Halsey died on August 20, 1959 on Fishers Island in New York. He is buried in Arlington National Cemetery.

BILL COSBY

William Henry Cosby, Jr. was born on July 12, 1937 in Philadelphia, Pennsylvania. His mother was a maid and his father was a cook in the U. S. Navy. He was one of four brothers and was raised in Philadelphia.

In elementary school he was the captain of the baseball and track and field teams as well as class president. In high school he played football, basketball, baseball, and ran track. After school he worked selling produce, shining shoes, and stocking shelves at a supermarket to help the family. He eventually dropped out of high school and joined the Navy as a Hospital Corpsman for four years. While in the Navy he earned his high school diploma via correspondence courses. After discharge from the Navy he entered Temple University in Philadelphia on a track and field scholarship. He was also the fullback on the football team.

Bill left Temple to pursue a career in comedy, though he would return to complete his studies in the 1970s. He received national exposure on NBC's *The Tonight Show* in the summer of 1963 and released *Bill Cosby Is a Very Funny Fellow... Right,* the first of a series of popular comedy albums in 1964. In 1965, when he was cast alongside Robert

Culp in the *I Spy* espionage adventure series, he became the first African-American co-star in a dramatic television series. In 1972, Bill received an MA from the University of Massachusetts and was also back in prime time with a variety series. His greatest television success came in September, 1984 with the debut of *The Cosby Show*. It went on to become the highest ranking sitcom of all time. Bill Cosby has been awarded four Emmys, nine Grammys, and numerous other honors.

JOHN AMOS

John Amos was born on December 27, 1939 in Newark, New Jersey, the son of Annabelle and John A. Amos. John, Sr. was an automobile mechanic by trade.

John, Jr. graduated from East Orange High School in 1958 and enrolled at Long Beach City College the same year. He later transferred to Colorado State University. John was Golden Gloves boxing champion and also played football for the university. In 1964 he signed a free agent contract with the American Football League's Denver Broncos. He was released before the season and played with Joliet Explorers of the United Football League. In 1965 he played for the Norfolk Neptunes and Wheeling Ironmen of the Continental Football League. In 1966 he played with the Jersey City Jets and Waterbury Orbits of the Atlantic Coast Football League. In 1967 he signed a free agent contract with the American Football League's Kansas City Chiefs. He eventually wound up his career with the Victoria Steelers of the Continental Football League, where he ended his football career in 1967.

John went into acting and joined *The Mary Tyler Moore Show* on television as Gordy Howard the weatherman from 1970 to 1973. He then played James Evans, the husband of

Florida Evans, in *Good Times*. John ended his role as James Evans and then was part of the Emmy award winning *Roots*, playing the adult Kunta Kinte in 1977. John has starred in other television series and has had film roles in *Coming to America, Vanishing Point, The Beastmaster*, and *Die Hard 2*. John has the distinction of winning more TV Land Awards than anyone.

TOMMY LEE JONES

Tommy Lee Jones was born on September 15, 1946 in San Saba, Texas, the son of Clyde C. Jones, an oil field worker, and Lucille Marie (nee Scott), a police officer, school teacher, and beauty shop owner. The two were married and divorced twice. Jones, an eighth-generation Texan, had a Cherokee grandparent.

After attending Robert E. Lee High School, Tommy Lee entered Harvard on a need-based scholarship, staying in Mower B-12 as a freshman, across the hall from future Vice President Al Gore. As an upperclassman he became a roommate to Al Gore.

Tommy Lee was an outstanding football player and played offensive guard on Harvard's undefeated 1968 team. He was nominated as a first team All-Ivy League and played in the memorable and literal last-minute Harvard sixteen-point comeback to tie Yale in the 1968 game. Tommy Lee graduated cum laude with a BA degree in English in 1969. He was enshrined on the All-Time Harvard team in recent years.

After graduation he moved to New York City to become an actor, making his Broadway debut in *A Patriot for Me* in 1969. In 1970 he landed his first film role, appropriately playing a Harvard student in *Love Story*. Since beginning his career as an actor he has starred in *The Fugitive, U.S. Marshalls, Batman Forever, Under Siege, Men in Black, Lonesome Dove, No Country for Old Men, Man of the House*, and *The Three Burials of Melquiades Estrada*. He has also portrayed real-life figures Howard Hughes, executed murderer Gary Gilmore, and baseball great Ty Cobb. He has won Emmys, Golden Globes, and two Academy Awards, and has been nominated numerous times for these and other awards.

CHUCK CONNORS

Chuck Connors was born Kevin Joseph Aloysius Connors on April 10, 1921 in Brooklyn, New York, the son of Allan and Marcella Connors, immigrants from the Dominion of New-foundland. His father was a longshoreman and his mother a homemaker. He was reared Roman Catholic and served as an altar boy at the Basilica of Our Lady of Perpetual Help in Brooklyn.

His athletic talents earned him a scholarship to the private high school Adelphi Academy, and then to the Catholic college, Seton Hall University in South Orange, New Jersey. He left college after two years and enlisted in the Army in 1942. He spent most of the war as a tank warfare instructor, stationed at Camp Campbell, Kentucky and later at West Point, New York.

Following his military discharge in 1946 he joined the newly-formed Boston Celtics of the Basketball Association of America. He played for numerous minor league teams before joining the Dodgers in 1949. He played only one game for the Dodgers before being traded to the Chicago Cubs, where he played in 66 games as a first baseman. He is one of only 12 athletes in history to have played for both Major League Baseball and the NBA.

After baseball Chuck became an actor where he achieved stardom, primarily for his role as Lucas McCain in the ABC television Western *The Rifleman*. In 1991 he was inducted into the Western Performers Hall of Fame at the National Cowboy and Western Heritage Museum in Oklahoma City.

Chuck Connors died at the age of 71 in Los Angeles of pneumonia stemming from lung cancer.

ESTHER WILLIAMS

Ester Jane Williams was born on August 8, 1921 in Inglewood, California. She was the fifth and youngest child of Louis Stanton Williams and Bula Myrtle Gilpin. Louis was a sign painter and Bula was a psychologist. The two lived on neighboring farms in Kansas and carried on a nine year courtship before they married and moved to California.

Ester was enthusiastic about swimming in her youth. Her older sister, Maurine, took her to the beach and the local pool. She took a job counting towels at the pool to pay the five cent entry fee, and while there, had swimming lessons from the male lifeguards. From them she learned the "male only" swimming strokes, including the butterfly breaststroke, with which she would later break records. Her medley team set the record for the 300-yard relay at the Los Angeles Athletic Club in 1939. She was also National AAU champion in the 100 meter freestyle. Ester planned to compete in the 1940 Summer Olympics but it was canceled when World War II started.

Esther graduated from Washington Preparatory High School in 1939. During her senior year in high school she enrolled in Los Angeles City College to retake a high school course in which she had made a bad grade. To earn money to pay tuition she took a job as a stock girl at I. Magnin Department Store where she also modeled clothing for customers. While working at I. Magnin, she was contacted by Billy Rose's assistant and asked to audition as a replacement for Eleanor Holm in his Aquacade show. She won the role and stayed with the show until it closed in September, 1940. She had been spotted by MGM scouts while doing the Aquacade and was offer a contract. She went on become a major film star.

JOHNNY MATHIS

Johnny Mathis was born on September 30, 1935 in Gilmer, Texas, the fourth of seven children to Clem Mathis and his wife Mildred Boyd, and is of both African-American and Caucasian descent. The family moved when he was young to San Francisco, California on Post Street, in the famous Fillmore district where he was raised.

His father worked for a time in vaudeville, and when he saw the budding talent in his son, the elder Mathis bought an old upright piano for $25 to encourage his efforts. From his father, Johnny began learning songs and routines and started singing and dancing for visitors at home and later publicly at school and church events. At thirteen he was taken to Connie Cox, a San Francisco Bay Area voice teacher, who accepted him as a student in exchange for work he would do around her house. He studied with Cox for six years and remains one of the few popular singers to have had professional voice training.

At George Washington High School Johnny was well known not only for his singing abilities, but also as a star athlete. On the track and filed team, he was a high jumper and hurdler, and on the basketball team, he earned four athletic letters. In 1954 he enrolled at San Francisco State University on a scholarship with the intention of becoming an English and physical education teacher.

In 1955 Johnny was offered a recording contract with Columbia Records and at the same time had a chance to go to the Olympic tryouts to which he had been invited. He made the decision to sign with Columbia and the rest is history. He received the Lifetime Achievement Award in 2003 and he was inducted into the Grammy Hall of Fame. He has sold more than 180 million records worldwide.

NICK NOLTE

Nicholas King "Nick" Nolte was born on February 8, 1941 in Omaha, Nebraska, the son of Helen, a department store buyer, and Franklin A. Nolte, a farmer's son who worked in irrigation pump sales and who was an All-American football player at Iowa State University in 1934. Nick's father was of German descent; his maternal grandfather, Matthew Leander King, invented the hollow-tile silo and was prominent in early aviation.

Nick went to Omaha Benson High School, where he was the kicker on the football team. He got kicked out of Benson for digging a hole and hiding beer before a practice session. After his expulsion, he attended Westside High School from which he graduated. He went on to attend Arizona State University on a football scholarship and then to Eastern Arizona College. At Eastern Arizona he lettered in football as a tight end and defensive end, in basketball as a forward, and as a catcher on the baseball team. Poor grades eventually ended his future in college so he began a career in acting.

Nick became a model in the late 1960s and early 1970s. He appeared in a national magazine advertisement in 1972 entitled "Summer Blonde" sitting on a log next to a blonde

Sigourney Weaver. He landed his first big acting role in the TV production of *Rich Man, Poor Man* in 1976. Since then he has had a successful career playing a wide variety of characters in more than 40 films. In 1991 he would receive his first nomination for the Academy Award for Best Actor for his role in *Prince of Tides.* He has been awarded the Los Angeles Film Critics Association Award for Best Actor, Golden Globe Award, New York Film Critics Award, and the National Society of Film Critics Award.

BOB HOPE

Leslie Townes Hope was born on May 29, 1903 in Eltham, London, England, the fifth of seven sons. His father, William Henry Hope, was a stonemason and his Welsh mother, Avis, was a light opera singer who later worked as a cleaning woman. The family moved to Cleveland, Ohio in 1908 and Bob became a U. S. citizen in 1920 at the age of seventeen. From the age of 12, he worked at a variety of odd jobs at a local boardwalk doing dance and comedy patter to make extra money. He entered many dancing and amateur talent contests and won prizes for an impersonation of Charlie Chaplin. He also boxed briefly and unsuccessfully under the name Packy East, once making it to the semifinals of the Ohio novice championship.

In 1918 at the age of 15 he was admitted to the Boys Industrial School in Lancaster, Ohio, formerly known as the Ohio Reform School. Silent film comedian Fatty Arbuckle saw one of his performances with his first partner, Lloyd "Lefty" Durbin, and in 1925 got the pair steady work with Hurley's Jolly Follies. In 1929 he changed his first name to "Bob" because he wanted a name with a friendly "Hiya fellas" sound to it. After five years on the vaudeville circuit Bob was surprised and humbled when he and his partner and future wife Grace Louis Troxell (he would later divorce Grace and marry Delores in 1934) failed a 1930 screen test for Pathe at Culver City, California.

Bob would later go on to become one of the most successful and beloved comedians of all time. On radio shows, in movies, and in USO tours, he entertained millions. Even when he stopped dancing, he stayed active as a golfer. Bob Hope died at the age of 100 on July 27, 2003 at his home in Toluca Lake, California. He was interred in the Bob Hope Memorial Garden at San Fernando Mission Cemetery in Los Angeles, where his mother is also buried.

GERALD FORD

Gerald Rudolph Ford, Jr. was born Leslie Lynch King, Jr. on July 14, 1913 in Omaha, Nebraska, where his parents lived with his paternal grandparents. His father was Leslie Lynch King, Sr., a wool trader and son of prominent banker Charles Henry King. His mother was the former Dorothy Ayer Gardner who separated from King Sr. just sixteen days after her son's birth. She took her son with her to Oak Park, Illinois, home of her sister. From there she moved to the home of her parents, Levi Gardner and his wife Adele in Grand Rapids, Michigan. Dorothy divorced King in December, 1913. On February 1, 1916 she married Gerald Rudolph Ford, a salesman in a family owned paint and varnish company. They then called her son Gerald Rudolph Ford, Jr. The future president was never formally adopted, however, and he did not legally change his name until December 3, 1935.

He was raised in Grand Rapids and attended Grand Rapids South High School, where he was a star athlete and captain of the football team. In 1930 he was selected to the All-City team and attracted the attention of many college recruiters. He then chose to attend the University of Michigan and played center and linebacker on the football team and helped the Wolverines to undefeated seasons and national titles in 1932 and 1933. His teammates later voted Ford their most valuable player. In 1934 he was selected to play in Shriner's East West Crippled Children game in San Francisco, and as part of the 1935 Collegiate All-Star football team, Ford played against the Chicago Bears in an exhibition game at Soldier Field.

By virtue of his eventual career as President of the United States, the University of Michigan retired his No. 48 jersey in 1994.

RICHARD NIXON

Richard Milhous Nixon was born on January 9, 1913, to Francis and Hannah Nixon in a house his father had built in Yorba Linda, California. His mother was a Quaker, and his upbringing was marked by conservative Quaker views of the time, such as refraining from drinking, dancing, and swearing. His father converted from Methodism to Quakerism after the marriage.

Richard's early life was marked by hardships. Two of his bothers died before he was 21 and his family's ranch failed in 1922. The Nixons then moved to Whittier, California, the home of his mother's relatives where his father opened a grocery store. Richard attended Fullerton High School in Fullerton, but later transferred to Whittier High School where he graduated second in his class in 1930. Financial concerns forced him to decline scholarships to Harvard and Yale universities. He then enrolled at Whittier College, a local Quaker school. He played both football and basketball and was a track runner.

He graduated second in his class from Whittier and received a full scholarship to Duke University School of Law.

He graduated third in his class in June 1937 and returned to California and was admitted to the bar that same year. He began practicing with Wingert and Bewley and handled litigation for local petroleum companies and other corporate matters. In June, 1940 he married Thelma "Pat" Ryan and in January 1042 moved to Washington, DC where he took a job with the Office of Price Administration. After Naval service in World War II he won a House of Representatives seat in 1946. He served as Vice President of the United States from 1953 to1961 and as President from 1969 to 1974 when he resigned. He died April 22, 1994.

GEORGE CLOONEY

George Clooney was born on May 6, 1961 in Lexington, Kentucky. His mother, Nina, was a former beauty pageant queen, and his father, Nick, was an anchorman plus game show and American Movie Classics host. Clooney is of Irish descent on his father's side. His paternal great-great grand-parents, Nicholas Clooney and Bridget Byron, emigrated to the U.S. from Ireland. He was raised a strict Roman Catholic. He has an older sister, Adelia, and his cousins include actors Miguel and Rafael Ferrer, who are the sons of his aunt, singer Rosemary Clooney, and actor Joe Ferrer. He is also related to another singer, Debby Boone, who married Jose Ferrer and Rosemary Clooney's son, Gabriel.

George began his education at the Blessed Sacrament School in Fort Mitchell, Kentucky. In middle school, George developed Bell's palsy, a debilitating condition that partially paralyzes the face. The malady went away within a year, for-tunately. His parents eventually moved to Augusta, Kentucky, where George attended Augusta High School. He was an enthusiastic baseball and basketball player and even tried out with the Cincinnati Reds in 1977 to play professional baseball, but was not offered a contract.

He attended Northern Kentucky University from 1979 to 1981 majoring in History and Political Science. He left college and began a career as an actor, winning his first role as an extra in the TV series *Centennial* in 1978. George went on to become an outstanding actor and won an Academy Award in 2006 for Best Supporting Actor for his work in the Middle East thriller *Syriana*.

RONALD REAGAN

Ronald Wilson Reagan was born on February 6, 1911 in an apartment on the second floor of a commercial building in Tampico, Illinois. His father was John Edward "Jack" Reagan and his mother was Nelle Wilson Reagan. Ronald's father was of Irish Catholic ancestry, while his mother had Scots-English ancestors. Ronald had one older brother, Neil "Moon" Reagan who became an advertising executive. As a boy Reagan's father nicknamed him "Dutch" due to his "fat little Dutchman" like appearance and his "Dutchboy" haircut. In late 1929, the Reagans moved to Dixon, where he attended Dixon High School and developed interest in acting, sports, and storytelling.

His first job was as a lifeguard at the Rock River in Lowell Park, near Dixon, in 1926. He is credited with saving 77 lives during his time as a lifeguard. After high school Ronald attended Eureka College, a small school sponsored by the Disciples, where he developed a reputation as jack of all trades, excelling in campus politics, sports and theater. He was a member of the football and track teams, the basketball cheerleading squad, captain of the swimming team, yearbook editor and was elected student body president.

After graduating from Eureka in 1932, Ronald got a job at the University of Iowa to broadcast home football games for the Hawkeyes. He later moved to WHO radio in Des Moines as an announcer for the Chicago Cubs baseball games. While traveling with the Cubs in California, Ronald took a screen test in 1937 that led to a seven-year contract with Warner Brothers studios. He did not serve in the military during World War Two. He went on to have an illustrious career in entertainment and politics. He was elected President of the United States in 1980 and served for two terms.

Ꞌ

GENE WILDER

Gene Wilder was born Jerome Silberman on June 11, 1933 in Milwaukee, Wisconsin, the son of Chicago-born Jeanne and William J. Silberman, a Russian Jewish immigrant. Gene first became interested in acting at age 8, when his mother was diagnosed with rheumatic fever and the doctor told him to "try and make her laugh." When Jeanne Silberman felt that her son's potential wasn't being fully realized in Wisconsin, she sent him to Black-Foxe, a military institute in Hollywood, where he wrote that he was bullied and sexually assaulted. After an unsuccessful short stay at Black-Foxe he returned home and became increasingly involved with the local theatre community. After graduating from high school he went to the University of Iowa and studied Communication and Theatre Arts.

Following graduation from Iowa, he was accepted at the Bristol Old Vic Theatre School in Bristol, England. After six months of studying fencing, Wilder became the first freshman to win the All-School Fencing Championship. Gene returned to the United States and was drafted into the Army on September 10, 1956.

In November 1957 his mother died from ovarian cancer and he was discharged from the army a year later. Gene was later accepted into the Actor's Studio at which time he changed his name to Wilder (from Thornton Wilder} and Gene (from Thomas Wolfe's first novel *Look Homeward Angel*). In 1963 Gene was cast as the lead actor in the Broadway play *Mother Courage and Her Children* with Anne Bancroft and her boy-friend Mel Brooks. Wilder and Brooks would later collaborate in such films as *The Producers, Young Frankenstein*, and *Blazing Saddles*. Gene was successful in the industry as an actor, singer, director, screenwriter, and author. He was married to Gilda Radner.

GEORGE H. W. BUSH

George Herbert Walker Bush was born on June 12, 1924 in Milton Massachusetts. The family moved to Greenwich, Connecticut shortly after his birth. He began his formal education in Greenwich and in 1936 attended Phillips Academy in Andover, Massachusetts where he was captain of both the varsity baseball and soccer teams.

Following the attack on Pearl Harbor in December, 1941, George decided to join the Navy, so after graduating from Phillips Academy in 1942, he became a naval aviator at the age of 18. After completing the 10-month course, he was commissioned as an ensign and assigned to Corpus Christi, Texas on June 9, 1943. The following year his squadron was based on the *USS San Jacinto* as a member of Air Group 51 in the south Pacific. On one mission against the Japanese his plane, a Grumman TBM Avenger, was hit by flak and his engine caught fire. He bailed out and was rescued by his ship's crew from the ocean. George was discharged from the Navy in 1945 and returned to the States where he married Barbara Pierce on January 6, 1945.

George had been accepted to Yale University prior to his enlistment and now took the offer. He was captain of the

Yale baseball team, and as a left-handed first baseman, played in the first two College World Series. As the team captain, George met Babe Ruth before a game during his senior year. He graduated from Yale in 1948 with a Bachelor's Degree in Economics. He went on to be a very successful businessman in Texas. He was elected Vice President under Ronald Reagan and served from 1981 to 1989. He was elected President of the United States in 1998 and served until 1993. He is currently retired and plays a lot of golf

GEORGE W. BUSH

George Walker Bush was born on July 6, 1946 in New Haven, Connecticut. He was the first child of George H. W. Bush and Barbara Bush. He was raised in Midland and Houston, Texas, with his four siblings, Jeb, Neil, Marvin, and Dorothy. Another younger sister, Robin, died from leukemia at the age of three in 1953. As a child, George attended public schools in Midland until his family moved to Houston after he completed seventh grade. George finished high school at Phillips Academy; a boarding school in Andover, Massachusetts where his father had gone.

George played baseball during his senior year and was also the head cheerleader. George then attended Yale University from 1964 to 1968, graduating with a Bachelor of Arts degree in History. While at Yale he was a keen rugby union player, and was on Yales's 1st Fifteen.

In May 1968, George was commissioned into the Texas Air National Guard. After two years of active-duty service while training, he was assigned to Houston, flying Conair F-102s with the 47th Fighter Interceptor Group. In October 1973 he was discharged from the Texas Air National Guard. Beginning in the fall of 1973 he attended the Harvard Business School, where he earned an MBA. On November 5, 1977 he married Laura Welch, a school teacher and librarian, in Midland, Texas. In 1978, George ran for the House of Representatives from Texas but lost the election. He returned to the oil industry and then moved his family to Washington, DC in 1988 to work on his father's campaign for President. In 1995 George was elected Governor of Texas and in 1994 elected to be the 43rd President of the United States. He served until January 20, 2009.

BURT REYNOLDS

Burton Leon "Burt" Reynolds, Jr. was born on February 11, 1936 in Lansing, Michigan. His parents were Burton Lee Reynolds, who was of Cherokee and Irish ancestry, and his wife Fern Miller. In 1946 the Reynolds moved to Riviera Beach, Florida where his father became Chief of Police. Riviera Beach is the next town north of West Palm Beach.

In his senior year at Palm Beach High School, Burt was named First Team All State and All Southern as a fullback, and received multiple scholarship offers. After graduating from high school he attended Florida State University on a college football scholarship and played halfback. He hoped to be named to All American teams, and to have a career in professional football. In the first game of the season, however, he was injured, and a car accident later that year worsened the injury.

With his college football career ended, Burt considered becoming a police officer, but his father suggested that he finish college and become a parole officer. In order to keep up with his studies be began taking classes at Palm Beach Junior College. While there he was asked to try out for an acting part in a play called *Outward Bound*. He won the lead role and won the 1956 Florida State Drama Award for his performance. The award included a scholarship to the Hyde Park Playhouse, a summer stock theater in New York. While at Hyde Park he met Joanne Woodward, who helped find him an agent.

Burt eventually won a film studio contract in Hollywood and went on to a highly successful career in movies and television. One of his most famous roles was as a football-playing convict in *The Longest Yard*. He is now one of America's most recognizable personalities with more than 90 feature films and 300 television episodes.

ROBERT REDFORD

Charles Robert Redford, Jr. was born on August 18, 1936 in Santa Monica, California, the son of Martha and Charles Robert Redford Sr. Robert is of English and Scots-Irish descent.

He attended Van Nuys High School in Los Angeles where he was a teammate of Don Drysdale on the Van Nuys High School baseball team. He graduated in 1954 and received a baseball scholarship to the University of Colorado, where he was a pitcher.

While at college Robert worked at the famous restaurant/bar The Sink. He later studied painting at the Pratt Institute in Brooklyn and took classes in theatrical set design at the American Academy of Dramatic Arts in New York City. On August 9, 1958 he married Lola Van Wagemen in Las Vegas. They had four children. The first son, Scott, died of sudden infant death syndrome on November 17, 1959. Robert and Lola divorced in 1985 and in 2009 he married his longtime partner, Sibylle Szaggars, at the luxurious Louis C. Jacob Hotel in Hamburg, Germany.

Robert's career began in New York where an actor could find work both in television and on stage. Starting in 1959 he appeared as a guest star on numerous television programs including *The Untouchables, Perry Mason, Alfred Hitchcock Presents, The Twilight Zone* and others. He earned an Emmy nomination as Best Supporting Actor for his performance in *The Voice of Charlie Pont* (ABC, 1962). He made his screen debut in 1962 in *War Hunt,* co-starring with John Saxon in a film set during the Korean War. Robert has received two Oscars, one for directing *Ordinary People* and one for Lifetime Achievement as an actor and director. He started the Sundance Film Festival (named for the character he played in *Butch Cassidy and the Sundance Kid*) to promote new and independent film makers.

JACK PALANCE

Volodymyr Palahnink, aka Jack Palance, was born on February 18, 1919 in the Lattimer Mines section of Hazle Township, Pennsylvania, the son of Anna and Ivan Palahnink, who was an anthracite coal miner. Palance's parents were Ukrainian immigrants, his father a native of Ivane Zolote in Southwestern Ukraine and his mother from the Lviv region.

Jack worked in coal mines during his youth before becoming a boxer. In the late 1930s, Jack started a professional boxing career, fighting under the name Jack Brazzo. He reportedly compiled a record of 15 consecutive victories with 12 knockouts before fighting the future heavyweight contender Joe Baksi in a "Pier-6" brawl, in which Jack lost in a close decision. With the outbreak of World War II, Jack's boxing career ended and his military career began. His rugged face, which took many beatings in the ring, was disfigured when he bailed out of a B-24 Liberator bomber while on a training flight in southern Arizona, where he was a student pilot. Plastic surgeons repaired the damage as best they could, but he was left with a distinctive, somewhat gaunt Look.

He was discharged from the Army Air Force in 1944. He then entered Stanford University and graduated in 1947 with a BA degree in Drama. His acting break came as Marlon Brando's understudy in *A Streetcar Named Desire* and he eventually replaced Brando on stage as Stanley Kowalski. During half a century of film and television appearances he was nominated for three Academy Awards, all as Best Actor in a Supporting Role, winning in 1991 for his role in *City Slickers*. He died on November 10, 2006 at the age of 87 in Montecito, California.

TOM SELLECK

Thomas William Selleck was born on January 29, 1945 in Detroit, Michigan, the son of Martha, a homemaker, and Robert, an executive and real estate investor. The family moved to Sherman Oaks, Los Angeles, California when Tom was growing up.

Tom graduated from Grant High School in Sherman Oaks in 1962 and then entered the University of California on a basketball scholarship. While at the university he also did modeling, and a drama coach suggested that he try acting. Upon graduating with a Bachelor's Degree in Business Administration, he studied acting at the Beverly Hills Play-house while serving in the 160th Infantry of the California National Guard. He was activated at the riot outbreaks in Watts and performed his duties as required.

Tom's first TV appearance was as a college senior on *The Dating Game* in 1965 and again in 1967. He lost both times. Soon thereafter he appeared in commercials for products such as Pepsi-Cola. He began his career with bit parts in small movies, including *Myra Breckinridge* and *The Seven Minutes*. He also appeared in a number of TV series, mini-series, and TV movies and had a recurring role on*The Rock-*

ford Files. Tom, after years of little interest, was cast as Thomas Magnum in *Magnum, P. I.* The producers of the show would not release the actor and he had to pass on the title role of Indiana Jones, which then went to Harrison Ford. The shooting of the pilot for *Magnum* was delayed for six months but when released in the early 1980s it made Tom an instant star. He continues to act and has turned to producing films. He is a favorite of fans everywhere.

CHARLEY PRIDE

Charley Frank Pride was born on March 18, 1938 in Sledge, Mississippi, one of eleven children of poor share-croppers. His father named him "Charl Frank Pride" but because of an error on his birth certificate, his legal name is Charley Frank Pride.

In his early teens he began playing guitar, but although he loved music, his life-long dream was to become a professional baseball player. In 1952 he pitched for the Memphis Red Sox of the Negro American League and he pitched well. In 1953 he signed a contract with the Boise Yankees, The Class C farm team of the New York Yankees. During that season, an injury caused him to lose the "mustard" on his fast-ball, and he was sent to the Yankees Class D team in Fond du Lac, Wisconsin. Later that season, while in the Negro Leagues with the Louisville Clippers, he and another player were traded to the Birmingham Black Barons for a team bus. He pitched for several other minor league teams and his career seemed to be advancing. He was then called into the military service for two years and when he was discharged he tried baseball again.

When it became apparent that he was not going to make it to the majors, he chose a music career. After struggling to get a contract with a record label, he finally caught the ear of record producer Chet Atkins at RCA Records. Chet had made stars out of country singers such as Jim Reeves, Skeeter Davis, and others. Charley signed with RCA in 1966. His great success came in the early-to-mid 1970s, when he was the best-selling performer since Elvis Presley. Charley is one of the few African-American country musicians to have success in the largely white country music industry and the only one to be inducted into the Grand Ole Opry.

BILLY RAY CYRUS

William Ray Cyrus was born on August 25, 1961 in Flatwoods, Kentucky to Ron Cyrus, a politician, and his wife, the former Ruth Ann Casto. His grandfather was a Pentecostal preacher. Growing up, he was surrounded by bluegrass and gospel music from his family. His father, a right-handed man, played guitar, but Billy Ray was a lefty, and could never learn to play the instrument.

He entered Georgetown College in Kentucky on a baseball scholarship before switching his interests to music.

From 1980 to 1990 he played at bars before getting a record deal with Mercury Nashville Records. While trying to get a recording contract in Los Angeles he was referred to as "too country," and in Nashville he was "too rock." However, in 1990, he signed a contract with PolyGram/Mercury and began to record and write music for his debut album. *Some Gave All* was released in 1992 and became an instant chart and sales success. It debuted as No. 1 on the Billboard Top Country Albums, Billboard 200, Canadian Country Albums chart, Canadian Albums chart, and several other foreign countries. The album featured four consecutive Top 40 singles on the Hot Country Singles & Tracks chart from 1992 to

1993. The most successful single released was Achy Breaky Heart. It reached No. 1 on the Hot Country Singles & Tracks chart and was also a hit on the pop charts, where it reached No. 4. Billy, a multi-platinum selling recording artist, has scored a total of eight top-ten singles on the U. S. Billboard Hot Country Songs chart. *Some Gave All* has been certified 9 times Multi-Platinum and holds the record for the longest time spent by a debut artist at No. 1.

LARRY GATLIN

Larry Wayne Gatlin was born on May 2, 1948 in Seminole, Texas. He was raised listening to country and gospel music. Even since childhood, he and his brothers, Steve and Rudy, have always sung and performed together. They sometimes performed on local radio stations, and occasionally on television shows. They also recorded a gospel music album for the Gospel label Sword and Shield.

After graduating from Odessa High School in 1966, Larry attended college at the University of Houston. A wide receiver on the football team, he caught a touchdown pass in a game in which the University of Houston scored 100 points.

He later was auditioning to join a gospel music group called the Imperials. The Imperials went on to perform in Las Vega in January 1971 at Jimmy Dean's Las Vegas Review. While walking through the showroom, he caught legendary country singer Dottie West's attention. She was so impressed with his songwriting skills that she recorded two of his compositions. She also passed one of his demo tapes around Nashville, Tennessee, and even arranged for him to relocate there. With West's help Larry found work in Nashville as a background singer for Kris Kristofferson. In 1973, he released his first album, *The Pilgrim*. Two singles were released from the album, "Sweet Becky Walker" and "Bitter They Are, Harder they Fall," however, both singles failed. A year later came the release of a new album *Rain/Rainbow* and a new song "Delta Dirt." The album and single proved very successful. The Gatlin Brothers made their first appearance on Larry's 1976 album and they went on to a very substantial career after that.

JOHNNY HORTON

John Gale Horton was born on April 30, 1925 in Los Angeles to John and Claudia Horton, the youngest of five children, but he was raised in the town of Rusk in East Texas. His family trekked back and forth from California often as migrant fruit pickers but always returned to the Rusk/Gallatin area in Texas.

After graduation from Gallatin High School in 1944, he attended the Methodist-affiliated Lon Morris College in Jacksonville, Texas on a basketball scholarship. He later attended Seattle University and also briefly he attended Baylor University, although he did not graduate from any college. Thereafter, he worked in California and Alaska.

He returned to Texas and won a talent contest hosted by then-radio announcer Jim Reeves at the Reo Palm Isle Club in Longview. He soon starred in the popular "Louisiana Hayride" in Shreveport. Johnny was an American country music singer who was most famous for his semi-folk, so-called "saga songs" which launched the "historical ballad" craze in the late 1950s and early 1960s. He had several major hits, most notably in 1959 with "The Battle of New Orleans" which won the 1959 Grammy Award for Best County & Western

Recording. The song won the Grammy Hall of Fame Award and in 2001 was named number 333 of the Songs of the Century. Other hits included "North to Alaska" and "Sink the Bismarck". Johnny Horton was killed in a head-on collision with a drunk driver on Highway 79 at Milano, Texas on November 5, 1960. When Johnny Cash, who was a food friend of Horton's, learned about the accident he said "I locked myself in one of the hotel's barrooms and cried."

KRIS
KRISTOFFERSON

Kristoffer "Kris" Kristofferson was born on June 22, 1936 in Brownsville, Texas, to parents Mary Ann and Lars Henry Kristofferson, a U.S. Army Air Corps major general. Like most "military brats," Kris moved around frequently as a youth, finally settling down in San Mateo, California, where he graduated from San Mateo High School.

An aspiring writer, Kris enrolled in Pomona College in 1954. He experienced his first dose of fame when he appeared in *Sports Illustrated*'s "Faces in the Crowd" for his achievements in collegiate rugby union, football, and track and field. He and fellow classmates revived the Claremont Colleges Rugby Club in 1958, which has remained a Southern California rugby dynasty. He graduated in 1958 with a BA, summa cum laude in Literature. Kris earned a Rhodes Scholarship to the University of Oxford and while at Oxford he was awarded his blue for boxing and began writing songs.

With the help of his manager, Larry Parnes, he recorded for Top Rank Records under the name Kris Carson. In 1960, Kris graduated with a BPhil in English literature and married an old girlfriend, Fran Beer. He ultimately joined the U. S. Army and achieved the rank of captain. He became a helicopter pilot and also attended Ranger School. In 1965. When his tour of duty ended, he was offered a position as a professor of English Literature at West Point, Instead, he decided to leave the Army and pursue songwriting professionally.

He went on to become a writer, singer-songwriter, actor, and musician. He is best known for hits such as "Me and Bobby McGee," "Sunday Mornin' Coming Down," and "Help me Make it Through the Night."

KATHARINE HEPBURN

Katharine Houghton Hepburn was born on May 12, 1907 in Hartford, Connecticut, the daughter of suffragette Katharine Martha Houghton (an heiress to the Corning Glass fortune and co-founder of Planned Parenthood) and Dr. Thomas Norval Hepburn, who was a successful urologist from Virginia with Maryland roots. She was of Scottish and English ancestry. Her siblings were Thomas, Richard, Robert, Marion, and Margaret.

Katharine's father insisted the girls practice swimming, riding, golf and tennis. Katherine, being eager to please her father, won a bronze medal for figure skating from the Madison Square Garden skating club, shot golf in the low eighties and reached the semi-final of the Connecticut Young Women's Golf Championship. She especially enjoyed swimming and regularly took dips in the frigid waters that fronted her bay front Connecticut home.

Katharine was educated at the Oxford School in West Hartford, Connecticut, before going on to Bryn Mawr College. She received a degree in history and philosophy in 1928, the same year she had her debut on Broadway after landing a bit part in *Night Hostess*. Katharine Hepburn went on to an outstanding career in film, television, and stage. Philip Barry wrote plays specifically for her, including *The Philadelphia Story*. She holds the record for the most Best Actress Oscar wins with four, from 12 nominations. She won an Emmy Award in 1976 for her lead role in *Love Among the Ruins*, and was nominated for four other Emmys, two Tony Awards, and eight Golden Globes. In 1999, the American Film Institute ranked Hepburn as the greatest female star in the history of American cinema. She died on June 29, 2003 at the age of 96 in Fenwick, Old Saybrook, Connecticut.

JOE BIDEN

Joseph Robinette "Joe" Biden, Jr. was born on November 20, 1942 in Scranton, Pennsylvania, the son of Joseph Biden Sr. and Catherine Eugenia Finnegan. He was the first of four siblings in an Irish Catholic family with roots in County Londonderry. His great-grandfather, Edward F. Blewitt, was a member of the Pennsylvania State Senate. Biden's father had been very well-off earlier in his life, but had suffered several business reverses by the time Joe was born.

In 1953, the Biden family moved to Wilmington, Delaware where Joe attended the Archmere Academy in Claymont. There he was a standout halfback/wide receiver on the high school football team. He helped lead a perennially losing team to an undefeated season in his senior year. He also played baseball in high school. He graduated from high school in 1961 and then attended the University of Delaware in Newark. He played halfback with the Blue Hens freshman football team, but he dropped a junior year plan to play for the varsity team as a defensive back.

He graduated with a BA degree in History and Political Science in 1965. He went on to receive his Juris Doctor from Syracuse University College of Law in 1968. Joe married

Neilia Hunter on August 27, 1966 and they later had three children. In 1969 Joe began practicing law in Wilmington, Delaware, first as a public defender and then with his own firm Biden and Walsh. Corporate law did not appeal to him so he ran for the 1972 U. S. Senate and he won the November 7, 1972 election in an upset. That began his political career. He is currently serving as the Vice President of the United States.

JESSE JACKSON

Jesse Louis Jackson was born on October 8, 1941 in Greenville, South Carolina, to Helen Burns, a 16-year old single mother. His biological father, Noah Louis Robinson, a former professional boxer and a prominent figure in the black community, was married to another woman when Jesse was born. He was not involved in his son's life. In 1943, his mother married Charles Henry Jackson, who would adopt Jesse 14 years later.

Jesse attended Sterling High School, a segregated school in Greenville, where he was a student athlete. Upon graduating in 1959, he rejected a contract from a professional baseball team so that he could attend the University of Illinois on a football scholarship.

One year later, however, Jesse transferred to North Carolina A&T located in Greensboro, North Carolina. Following his graduation from A&T, he attended the Chicago Theological Seminary with the intent of becoming a minister but dropped out in 1966 to focus full-time on the civil rights movement. In 1965, he participated in the Selma to Montgomery marches organized by Dr. Martin Luther King, Jr. and others. He was ordained in 1968, without a theological degree, awarded an honorary theological doctorate from Chicago in 1990, and received his Master of Divinity Degree in 2000. Jesse went on to be a candidate for the Democratic presidential nomination in 1984 and 1988 and served as a shadow senator for the District of Columbian from 1991 to 1997. He was the founder of both entities that merged to form Rainbow/PUSH. The Black Voices poll in February 2006 named him "the most important black leader."

JAMIE FOXX

Eric Marion Bishop was born on December 13, 1967 in Terrell, Texas. He is the son of Louise Annette Talley Dixon and Darrell Bishop. He was abandoned seven months after birth and was raised in Terrell by his mother's adoptive parents, Estelle and Mark Talley. Terrell was a racially segregated community at the time. Jamie had a strict Baptist upbringing and began piano lessons at the age of five.

Jamie attended Terrell High School, where he received top grades, played basketball and football as quarterback, and had an ambition to play for the Dallas Cowboys. He was the first player in the school's history to pass for more than 1,000 yards.

After completing high school, Jamie received a scholarship to United States International University, where he studied classical music and composition. After accepting a dare from a girl friend, he told jokes and did impressions at a comedy club's open mike night in 1989. When he found that female comedians were often called first to perform, he changed his name to Jamie Foxx, feeling that it was an ambiguous enough name to disallow any biases. He chose his surname as a tribute to comedian Redd Foxx.

Jamie joined the cast of *In Living Color* in 1991, and subsequently played a recurring role in the comedy-drama sitcom *Roc*. From 1996 to 2001, he starred in his own sitcom *The Jamie Foxx Show*, and in 1992 he made his film debut. As an actor, his work in the biographical film *Ray* earned him the Academy Award and BAFTA Award for Best Actor as well as the Golden Globe Award for Best Actor in a musical/comedy. He is also a Grammy Award winning musician, producing two albums which have charted highly on the Billboard 200.

JAMES CAAN

James Caan was born on March 26, 1940 in the Bronx, New York City, the son of Sophie and Arthur Caan, Jewish refugees from Germany. His father was a meat dealer. James grew up in Sunnyside, Queens, New York City, and was educated at P.S.150 40-01 on 43rd Avenue School in Queens.

After graduation from high school he attended Michigan State University where he played football. He later transferred to Hofstra University in Hampstead, New York, but did not graduate.

While studying at Hofstra, he became intrigued by acting. He was interviewed for, and accepted to, and graduated from New York City's Neighborhood Playhouse School of the Theatre. He began his acting career in television on such series as *The Untouchables, The Alfred Hitchcock Hour', Suspense Theatre, Combat, Ben Casey,* and *Dr. Kildare.* He had good parts in many films with such stars as John Wayne, Robert Mitchum, and Olivia de Havilland. In 1970, he won acclaim as dying football player Brian Piccolo in the television movie *Brian's Song.* The following year he was cast as mobster Sonny Corleone in *The Godfather.* He was nominated for an Academy Award for his performance in the film. From 1971 to 1982, James appeared in many films, playing a wide variety of roles in *T. R. Baskin, Cinderella Liberty, Freebie and the Bean, The Godfather Part II, Rollerball,* and others. From 1982 to 1987, James suffered from depression over his sister's death, a growing problem with cocaine, and "Hollywood burnout," and did not act in any films. He is currently very active in films and television.

DENZEL WASHINGTON

Denzel Hayes Washington, Jr. was born on December 28, 1954 in Mount Vernon, near New York City. His mother, Lennis, was a beauty parlor owner and operator born in Georgia and partly raised in Harlem. His father, Reverent Denzel Washington, Sr., was an ordained Pentecostal minister who also worked for the Water Department and at a local department store, S. Klein.

Denzel Jr. attended grammar school at Pennington-Grimes Elementary School in Mount Vernon until 1968 when he was sent to a private preparatory school, Oakland Military Academy in New Windsor, New York a the age of 14. He next attended Mainland High School, a public high school in Dayton Beach, Florida.

After high school Denzel attended Fordham University where he played collegiate basketball as a Freshman guard under coach P. J. Carlesimo.

Upon graduation from Fordham in 1977 with a B.A. in Drama and Journalism he was given a scholarship to attend graduate school at the American Conservatory Theatre in San Francisco where he stayed for one year before returning to New York to begin a professional acting career. He spent the summer of 1976 in St. Mary's City, Maryland in summer stock.

He made his professional acting debut in the 1977 made-for-television movie *Wilma* and his first Hollywood appearance in the 1981 film *Carbon Copy*. He has earned critical acclaim for his work in film since the 1990s. He has been awarded three Golden Glove awards and two Academy Awards, the first for his role in *Glory*, about a regiment of black soldiers fighting in the Civil War. He is notable as the second African American man (after Sidney Poitier) to win the Academy Award for Best Actor, which he received for his role in the 2001 film *Training Day*.

BOB BARKER

Robert William "Bob" Barker was born on December 12, 1923 in Darrington, Washington, and spent most of his youth on the Rosebud Indian Reservation in South Dakota. His mother, Matilda Valandra was a school teacher and his father, Byron John Barker, was the foreman on the electrical high line through the state of Washington. He is one-eighth Native American (Sioux). While in Washington, his father fell from a tower and was killed in 1929.

In 1931, the family moved to Springfield, Missouri, where Bob graduated from Central High School in 1941. He then attended Drury College in Springfield, on a basketball scholarship. His education was interrupted by World War II, during which he trained in the Navy s a fighter pilot. However, the war ended before he was assigned to a seagoing squadron. After the war, he returned to Drury to finish his education, graduating summa cum laude with a degree in economics.

Bob left Springfield and worked at a radio station in Florida before landing another radio job in California. He was hosting an audience-participation radio show in Los Angeles when game show producer Ralph Edwards happened to be listening and liked Bob's voice and style. Bob started hosting *Truth or Consequences* in 1956 and continued until 1975. He is best known for hosting CBS's *The Price is Right* from 1972 to 2007, making it the longest-running daytime game show in North American television history. After holding the job for 35 years and being in television for 50 years, he retired in June 2007. He has been a long-time supporter of animal rights, and of animal-rights activism, including groups such as the United Activists for Animal Rights and the Sea Shepherd Conservation Society.

BYRON "WHIZZER" WHITE

Byron Raymond "Whizzer" White was born on June 8, 1917 in Fort Collins, Colorado. He was raised in the nearby town of Wellington, Colorado, where he received a high school diploma in 1930.

After graduating at the top of his class at Wellington High School, he attended the University of Colorado on a football scholarship. He was an All-American halfback for the Colorado Buffaloes where he acquired the nickname "Whizzer" from a newspaper columnist. The nickname would follow him throughout his career. He also played basketball and baseball while at Colorado. He graduated in 1938 and won a Rhodes Scholarship to the University of Oxford, but deferred for a year so that he could play pro football. He signed a contract with the NFL's Pittsburgh Pirates (now Steelers). He led the league in rushing in his rookie season and became the game's highest-paid player. After graduating from Oxford, he played football for the Detroit Lions from 1940 to 1941. In three NFL seasons, he played in 33 games and was one of the first "big money" NFL players, making $15,000 a year. His career was cut short when he entered the United States Navy during World War II.

After the war he elected to attend law school at Yale rather than return to football. He was later appointed to the Supreme Court by President John F. Kennedy in 1962, and served until his retirement in 1993. He was elected to the College Football Hall of Fame in 1954. He died in Denver at the age of 84 from complications of pneumonia on April 15, 2002. He was the first and only Supreme Court Justice from the state of Colorado.

JAMES STEWART

James Maitland "Jimmy" Stewart was born on May 20, 1908 in Indiana, Pennsylvania, the son of Elizabeth and Alexander Stewart, who owned a hardware store.

Jimmy attended Mercersburg Academy prep school, graduating in 1928. At Mercersburg, Jimmy was active in a variety of activities. He was on the football and track teams. He was art editor for the yearbook and member of the choir club, glee club, and others.

He enrolled at Princeton in 1928. There, he excelled at studying architecture, so impressing his professors with his thesis on an airport design that he was awarded a scholarship for graduate studies, but he became attracted to the school's drama and music clubs. Upon graduation from Princeton in 1932, Jimmy joined the University Players on Cape Cod where he became good friends with Henry Fonda. They shared an apartment with Joshua Logan and Myron McCormick. Jimmy debuted on Broadway as a chauffeur in the comedy "*Goodbye Again*", in which he had two lines. In the fall of 1934, Fonda's success in "*The Farmer Takes A Wife*" took him to Hollywood. Jimmy attracted the interest of MGM scout Bill Grady. He took a screen test and signed a contract with MGM in April 1935, as a contract player for up to seven years at $350 a week.

Over the course of his career he was nominated for five Academy Awards, winning Best Supporting Actor for *The Philadelphia Story* and receiving the Lifetime Achievement award. He was a major MGM star and he also had a noted military career; he was a pilot in World War Two and rose to the rank of Brigadier General in the Air Force Reserve. He died on July 2, 1997 at the age of 89, in Los Angeles. Jimmy is one of the most beloved Hollywood personalities of all time.

RICHARD GERE

Richard Tiffany Gere was born on August 31, 1949 in Philadelphia, Pennsylvania. He is a descendant of *Mayflower* pilgrims Francis Eaton, John Billington, George Soule, Richard Warren, Degory Priest, William Brewster and Francis Cooke. Richard's mother, Doris Anna, was a homemaker, and his father, Homer George Gere, was an insurance agent for the Nationwide Mutual Insurance Company who had originally intended to become a minister.

In 1967 Richard graduated from North Syracuse Central High School, where he excelled at gymnastics and music, playing the trumpet. He attended the University of Massachusetts Amherst on a gymnastic scholarship, majoring in philosophy, but did not graduate, leaving after two years.

He first worked professionally at the Provincetown Playhouse on Cape Cod in 1971 where he starred in *"Rosencrantz and Guildenstern Are Dead"*. His first major acting role was in the original London stage version of *"Grease"* in 1973. He began appearing in Hollywood films in the mid 1970s, co-starring with Diane Keaton in the thriller *"Looking for Mr. Goodbar"* in 1977 and playing the leading role in director

Terrence Malick's well-reviewed 1978 film, *"Days of Heaven"*. He came to prominence in 1980 for his role in the film *"American Gigolo"*, which established him as a leading man and a sex symbol. He went on to star in several hit films including *"An Officer and a Gentleman"*, *"Pretty Woman"*, *"Primal Fear"*, and *"Chicago"*, for which he won a Golden Globe Award as Best Actor, as well as a Screen Actors Guild Award as part of the Best Cast. Richard Gere is also a political activist on behalf of refugees from Tibet.

ROBERT URICH

Robert Urich was born on December 19, 1946 in the small town of Toronto, Ohio. He was of Russian and Slovak extraction and raised as Roman Catholic.

Robert attended Florida State University on a football scholarship. In 1968, he earned a bachelor's degree in Radio and Television Communications. He went on to Michigan State University after working in Ohio to earn a master's degree in Broadcast Research and Management.

Robert was first married to actress Barbara Rucker (1968-74) and then to actress Heather Menzies in 1975; they remained married until his death in 2002. Between 1973 and just prior to his death, he had lead or supporting roles in no less than 19 television series and miniseries. He also regularly hosted National Geographic TV specials and the National Geographic Explorer documentary series. He was the guest host of *Saturday Night Live* in March 1982. He made a noteworthy screen appearance opposite Clint Eastwood in the 1973 file *Magnum Force* playing a vigilante motorcycle-patrol police officer. He was the spokesperson for Bayer Aspirin in 1990 and for Purina dog food in 2000. Most of his

TV series were short-lived, although several, such s *Vega$* and *Spencer for Hire*, proved to be successes. He played a main character, Jake Spoon, in the acclaimed television miniseries *Lonesome Dove*, a role for which he received many positive reviews. In 1996, Robert announced that he had been diagnosed with a rare form of cancer, synovial cell sarcoma, that attacks a person's joints. He continued to appear in film and TV during treatment. He ultimately died from the disease on April 16, 2002 at the age of 55 in Thousand Oaks, California.

JOHN ROBERTS

John Glover Roberts, Jr. was born on January 27, 1955 in Buffalo, New York, the son of John Glover Roberts, Sr. and Rosemary. All of his maternal great-grandparents were from Czechoslovakia. His father was a plant manager with Bethlehem Steel.

When John was in the fourth grade, his family moved to the beachside town of Long Beach, Indiana. He grew up with three sisters. He attended Note Dame Elementary School, a Roman Catholic grade school in Long Beach, and then La Lumiere School in LaPorte, Indiana and was an excellent student and athlete. He was captain of his football team and was a Regional Champion in wrestling. He also served on the athletic council and the Executive Committee of the Student Council and was also valedictorian.

He attended Harvard College, graduating with an A.B. in history summa cum laude in three years. He then attended Harvard Law School, and was the managing editor of the Harvard Law Review. He graduated from law school with his J.D. magna cum laude in 1979.After being admitted to the bar, he served as a law clerk for William Rehnquist before taking a position in the Attorney General's office during, the Reagan Administration. He went on to serve the Reagan Administration and the George H. W. Bush Administration in the Department of Justice and the Office of the White House Counsel. He was nominated for the Supreme Court by President George W. Bush in 2005 after the death of Chief Justice William Rehnquist.. He professes a conservative judicial philosophy in his jurisprudence.

JIM BUNNING

James Paul David "Jim" Bunning was born on October 23, 1931 in Southgate, Kentucky, the son of Gladys and Louis Aloysius Bunning. He graduated fro St. Xavier High School in Cincinnati in 1949 and later received a bachelor's degree in economics from Xavier University.

Jim's first game as a major league pitcher was on July 20, 1955, with the Detroit Tigers, after having toiled in the minor leagues until the 1955 season, when the Tigers club described him as having "an excellent curve ball," a confusing delivery and a sneaky fast ball. Jim pitched for the Detroit Tigers from 1955 to 1963 when he was traded to the Philadelphia Phillies. After 1967 he was traded to the Pittsburgh Pirates and then spent the 1969 season with the Los Angeles Dodgers. He then returned to the Phillies in 1970 and retired in 1971. He spent 17 seasons in the Major Leagues and when he retired, he had the second-highest total of career strikeouts in Major League history. He also pitched a perfect game in 1964, a feat that has been accomplished only nineteen times in Major League history. He was inducted into the Baseball Hall of Fame in 1996.

In 1986 he was elected to the U. S. House of Representatives from Kentucky and served from 1987 to 1999. He was elected to the U. S. Senate from Kentucky in 1998 and has served there since as the Republican junior U. S. Senator. Jim became the sixth oldest U. S. Senator and the oldest Republican in the Senate. In July 2009, he announced that he would not run for re-election in 2010.

ED O'NEIL

Edward Phillip "Ed" O'Neil, Jr. was born on April 12, 1946 into an Irish Catholic family in Youngstown, Ohio. His mother, Ruth Ann, was a homemaker and social worker, and his father, Edward Phillip O'Neil, Sr. was a steel mill worker and truck driver.

Ed attended Ursuline High School and went on to study at Ohio University in Athens, Ohio, and later at Youngstown State University where he played football. He was signed by the Pittsburgh Steelers in 1969 as an outside linebacker. He was released before the start of the 1969 regular season. Later, on *Married with Children*, he played a former high-school football star who had failed to make it big and constantly relived his glory days at Polk High. As part of this theme, former Pittsburgh Steelers great and Hall of Fame quarterback Terry Bradshaw made two guest appearances on the show.

Ed was a social studies teacher at Youngstown's Ursuline High School before becoming an actor. He played Lenny in a stage production of John Steinbeck's *Of Mice and Men* at the American Repertory Theater in Cambridge, Massachusetts. He made his film debut in John Boorman's *Deliverance* as a deputy. Ed is primarily known for playing the lead role of Al Bundy in *Married with Children*, a long running TV series. He is often cast as a police detective or FBI agent in television shows and films. He currently can be seen on the ABC sitcom *Modern Family* in the role of Jay Pritchett.

DICK GREGORY

Richard "Dick" Claxton Gregory was born on October 12, 1932 in St. Louis, Missouri.

As a poor student who excelled at running, Dick was aided by teachers at Sumner High School. He earned a track scholarship to Southern Illinois University in Carbondale. There he set school records as a half-miler and miler. His college career was interrupted for two years in 1954 when he was drafted into the U. S. Army.

The army was where he got his start in comedy, entering and winning several Army talent shows at the urging of his commanding officer. In 1956, Dick briefly returned to the university after his discharge, but soon left without a degree. In the hopes of performing comedy professionally, he moved to Chicago, where he became part of a new generation of black comedians that included Nipsey Russell, Bill Cosby, and Godfrey Cambridge. These comedians broke with the minstrel tradition, which presented stereotypical black characters. He performed in small, primarily black nightclubs while working for the United States Postal Service during the daytime. In 1961, while working at the black-owned Roberts

Show Bar in Chicago, he was hired by Hugh Hefner to work at the Chicago Playboy Club. Active in the civil rights movement, he came to Selma, Alabama and spoke for two hours on a public platform two days before "Freedom Day" on October 7, 1963.

Dick's first TV appearance was on the late night Jack Paar show. He soon began appearing nationally and on television and his 1964 autobiography, *Nigger*, sold ten million copies. Influenced to stand up for civil rights by his early surroundings of poverty and violence, he was one of the first comedians to successfully perform for both black and white audiences.

SAM WALTON

Samuel Moore "Sam" Walton was born on March 29, 1918 to Nancy and Thomas Gibson Walton near Kingfisher, Oklahoma. He lived with his parents on their farm until 1923. Sam's father decided farming did not generate enough income on which to raise a family, so he decided to go back to a previous profession as a mortgage man. He and his family moved to Chesterfield, Missouri. There they moved from one small town to another for several years. Growing up during the Great Depression, Sam had numerous chores to help make financial ends meet for his family.

While attending 8th grade in Shelbina, Sam became the youngest Eagle Scout in the state's history. He excelled at basketball and football during his high school years. After high school, he decide to attend college, hoping to find a better way to help support his family.

He attended the University of Missouri and majored in economics and was an ROTC officer. Upon graduating in 1940, he was voted "permanent president" of the class. He later joined JC Penney's as a management trainee in Des Moines, Iowa. He joined the U. S. Army Intelligence Corps, in 1942, supervising security at aircraft plants and prisoner of war camps. He reached the rank of captain. In 1945, after leaving the military, Sam opened a variety store. It was here that Sam pioneered many concepts that would prove to be crucial to his success. Later he would move to Bentonville, Arkansas where he would open Walton's Five and Dime. He went on to be the founder of Wal-Mart and Sam's Club and became an outstanding business success story. Sam died on April 5, 1992 at age 74 in Little Rock, Arkansas.

DONALD TRUMP

Donald John Trump was born June 14, 1946 in New York City. He is the son of Fred Christ Trump and his wife Mary. Donald was the fourth of five children of and his father was a wealthy real estate developer based in New York City. He was strongly influenced by his father in his eventual goals to make a career in real estate development.

Donald attended The Kew-Forest School in Forest Hills, Queens, but later his parents sent him to the New York Military Academy (NYMA). At NYMA in upstate New York, he earned academic honors, played varsity football in 1962, varsity soccer in 1963, and varsity baseball from 1962 – 64 (baseball captain '64). He was awarded the Coach's Award in baseball in 1964.

Donald attended Fordham University for two years before transferring to the Wharton School of the University of Pennsylvania. After graduating in 1968 with a Bachelor of Science in Economics, he joined his father's real estate company, the Trump Organization. His first project was the revitalization of the foreclosed Swifton Village apartment complex in Cincinnati, Ohio, clearing $6 million in profit. Starting with the renovation of the Commodore Hotel into the

Grand Hyatt, he continued with Trump Tower in New York City and several other residential projects. He would later expand into the airline industry (buying the Eastern Shuttle routes), and Atlantic City casino business, including buying the Taj Mahal Casino from the Crosby family. He is currently the Chairman and CEO of the Trump Organization. He is also the founder of Trump Entertainment Resorts. His extravagant lifestyle and outspoken manner have made him a celebrity for years. He is currently worth about $2 billion.

ALEC BALDWIN

Alexander Rae "Alec" Baldwin III was born on April 3, 1958 in Amityville, New York, the son of Carolyn Newcomb and Alexander Rae Baldwin, Jr. The senior Baldwin was a high school history and social studies teacher and football coach. Alec was raided in a Catholic family of Irish, English and French decent. He has three younger brothers, Daniel, William, and Stephen, who all became actors.

Alec attended Alfred G. Berner High School in Massapequa, Long Island and played football there under Coach Bob Reifsnyder, who is in the College Football Hall of Fame.

Alec attended George Washington University from 1976 to 1979 and then transferred to New York University (NYU) to study acting at the Lee Strasberg Theatre Institute. He returned to NY in 1994 and graduated with a Bachelor of Fine Arts Degree that same year. On May 12, 2010, he again returned to NYU, this time as a commencement speaker and to receive a Doctor of Fine Arts degree. Alec made his Broadway debut in 1986 and his credits include *Loot, Serious Money* and *A Streetcar Named Desire*. His first major acting role was as Billy Aldrich on the daytime soap opera *The Doc-*

tors. In 1984 to 1986 he starred in the television series *Knots Landing.* He has played both leading and supporting roles in films such as *Beetlejuice, The Hunt for Red October, The Aviator,* and *The Departed.* In 2003 he was nominated for an Academy Award for Best Supporting Actor in *The Cooler.* He currently stars as Jack Donaghy on the NBC sitcom *30 Rock.* He has received two Emmy Awards, three Golden Globe Awards, and four Screen Actors Guild Awards.

MICKEY ROURKE

Philip Andre "Mickey" Rourke Jr. was born on September 16, 1952 in Schenectady, New York to a family of Irish and French descent. His father, Philip, Sr., was an amateur body builder who left the family when Mickey was six years old. After his parents divorced, his mother, Ann, married Eugene Addis, a Miami Beach police officer with five sons, and moved Mickey and the family to southern Florida.

Mickey graduated from Miami Beach Senior High School in 1971. During his teenage years, Mickey focused his attention mainly on sports. He took up self-defense training and then later boxing. At age 12, Mickey won his first boxing match as a 118-pound bantamweight. He continued his boxing training at the famed 5th Street Gym, in Miami Beach, where Muhammad Ali began his boxing training. In 1968, he sparred with former World Welterweight Champion Luis Rodriguez who was rated as the number one middleweight boxer in the world. At the 1971 Florida Golden Gloves, Mickey suffered a concussion in the boxing ring and temporarily retired from the ring after compiling an amateur record of 20 wins, 17 by knockout, and 6 defeats.

Soon after giving up boxing he landed an acting role in a friend's production of *Deathwatch*. He then went to New York to study acting at the Actors Studio. His film debut was a small role in Steven Spielberg's film *1941*. He mostly appeared in television movies in his early career. He returned to boxing in the 1990s as a professional but soon returned to acting. He won a 2009 Golden Globe award and a BAFTA award, and was nominated for a Screen Actors Guild Award and an Academy Award for his work in the film *The Wrestler*.

JAMES DEAN

James Byron Dean was born on February 8, 1931; at the Seven Gables apartment house in Marion, Indiana to Winton Dean and Mildred Wilson. Six years after his father left farming to become a dental technician, Jimmy and his family moved to Santa Monica, California. The family spent several years there, and by all accounts young Jimmy was very close to his mother. He was enrolled at Brentwood Public School in the Brentwood neighborhood of Los Angles until his mother died of cancer when Jimmy was nine years old. Unable to care for his son, Winton Dean sent Jimmy to live with Winton's sister on a farm in Fairmount, Indiana, where he was raised in a Quaker background.

In high school, Jimmy's overall performance was mediocre. He was a popular school athlete, however, successfully playing on the baseball and basketball teams. After graduating from Fairmount High School on May 16, 1949, he moved back to California to live with his father and stepmother.

He enrolled in Santa Monica College and majored in pre-law but later transferred to UCLA and changed his major to drama. While at UCLA, he beat out 350 actors to land the role of Malcolm in *Macbeth*. At that time he also began acting with James Whitmore's acting workshop. Jimmy's first television appearance was in a Pepsi Cola television commercial. He would later gain enormous fame in the movies *Rebel Without a Cause, East of Eden,* and *Giant.* His enduring fame and popularity rests on only these three films. He died in a car wreck on September 30, 1955 in Cholame, California at the age of 24. He was the first actor to receive a posthumous Academy Award nomination for Best Actor.

ART LINKLETTER

Arthur Gordon "Art" Linkletter was born on July 17, 1912 in Moose Jaw, Saskatchewan, Canada. He revealed in his autobiography later in life that he had no contact with his natural parents or his sister or two brothers, since he was abandoned when only a few weeks old. He was adopted by May and Fulton John Linkletter, an evangelical preacher. When he was six, his family moved to San Diego, California where he graduated from high school at age 16.

During the early years of the Great Depression, he rode trains round the country doing odd jobs and meeting a wide variety of people. In 1934, he earned a bachelor's degree from San Diego State Teachers' College. While at San Diego State, he played for the basketball team and was a member of the swimming team.

He earned a degree in teaching, but took a job as a radio announcer at KGB in San Diego. In the 1940s, Art worked in Hollywood with John Guedel on their pioneering radio show, *People are Funny*. This became a television show in 1954 and ran until 1961. Other early television shows included *Life with Linkletter*, *Hollywood Talent Scouts*, and the film

Champagne for Caesar. He also guest-hosted *The Tonight Show* three times. In the 1950's Art became a major investor in the hula hoop. In 1963 he became the endorser and spokesman for Milton Bradley's Game of Life. He also hosted *House Party* which ran on CBS radio and television for 25 years. Art was famous for interviewing children on *House Party* and *Kids Say the Darndest Things* which led to a successful series of books. Art Linkletter died on May 26, 2010 in Los Angeles at the age of 97.

TOMMY SMOTHERS

Thomas Bolin Smothers III was born on February 2, 1937 in New York City, the son of Ruth, a homemaker, and Thomas B. Smothers, an army officer. After moving to California, he graduated from Redondo Union High School in Redondo Beach, California.

He was a competitive unicyclist, and a state champion gymnast in the parallel bars. He then attended San Jose State University.

Tom is a comedian, composer and musician, best know as half of the musical comedy team the Smothers Brothers, alongside his younger brother Dick. The Smothers Brothers made records and appeared on numerous television shows over the past few decades, including two variety shows of their own, *"The Smothers Brothers Show"* from 1965 to 1966, and *"The Smothers Brothers Comedy Hour'* in 1967. In motion pictures, Tom portrayed corporate-executive-turned-tap-dancing-magician Donald Beeman in one of his earlier films, *"Get to Know Your Rabbit"*. He also played a banker in *"Silver Bears.* In 1973, he voiced Ted E. Bear in the NBC animated Christmas special *"The Bear Who Slept Through*

Christmas". Ten years later, he voiced Ted E. Bear again for its Halloween sequel *"The Great Bear Scare"*. Tom also played guitar on John Lennon 's recording of his single "*Give Peace a Chance*". In 2008, during the 60th Primetime Emmy Awards, Tom was awarded a special Emmy. The award was presented by Steve Martin, a writer long ago on the Smothers Brothers show. Tom is now the owner of Remick Ridge Vineyards in Sonoma County, California with his wife Marcy Carriker and two children.

DEAN MARTIN

Dino Paul Crocetti (Dean Martin) was born on June 7, 1917 in Steubenville, Ohio to Italian immigrant parents, Gaetano and Angela Crocetti. His father was from Abruzo, Italy, and his mother was of part Neapolitan and part Sicilian ancestry.

He attended Grant Elementary School in Steubenville but eventually dropped out of high school in the 10th grade, He then got a variety of jobs: he delivered bootleg liquor, served as a speakeasy croupier, wrote crafty anecdotes, was a blackjack dealer, worked in a steel mill and boxed as a welterweight. He grew up a neighbor to Jimmy the Greek.

At the age of 15, he was a boxer who billed himself as "Kid Crochet". His prizefighting years earned him a broken nose, a scarred lip, and many sets of broken knuckles. Of his twelve bouts, he would later say "I won all but eleven."

Eventually, Dean gave up boxing and started singing with local bands, billed as "Dino Martini." Dean famously flopped at the Riobamba, a high class nightclub in New York, when he succeeded Frank Sinatra in 1943. Drafted into the Army in 1944 during World War II, he served a year stationed in

Akron, Ohio. By 1946 he was doing relatively well, but was still little more than an East Coast nightclub singer. In 1946, Dean teamed with comedian Jerry Lewis; they did slapstick, reeled off old vaudeville jokes, and did whatever else popped into their mind on the nightclub circuit. Martin and Lewis were the hottest act in America during the early 1950s before they broke up. Dean would then go on to have wonderful success with recordings, movies, and his own television show. Dean Martin died on December 25, 1995 in Beverly Hills at the age of 78.

TED DANSON

Edward Bridge "Ted" Danson III was born on December 29, 1947 in San Diego, California, the son of Jessica Danson and Edward Bridge Danson, Jr., an archeologist and museum director. The Dansons are of Scottish and English ancestry. Ted was raised in Flagstaff, Arizona.

In 1961, he enrolled in the prestigious Kent School where he was a basketball star.

He became interested in drama while attending Stanford University. He later transferred to the Carnegie Institute of Technology in Pittsburg, Pennsylvania, where he received his Bachelor of Fine Arts degree in Drama in 1972.

Ted began his television career as a contract player on daytime soap opera, *Somerset*. The played the role of Tom Conway from 1975 to 1976. He was also in a number of commercials, most recognizably as the Aramis man. He made a number of guest appearances in episodic television the late 1970s and early 1980s. In 1982, Ted was cast in his most recognizable role, as ex-baseball player and bartender Sam Malone on the hit sitcom *Cheers*. The show had a run of 11 seasons and its finale on May 20, 1993 was watched by 80 million people. It won four Emmy Awards for Outstanding Comedy Series and a Golden Globe for Best Series. The show ran from 1982 to 1993, with Ted receiving 11 consecutive Emmy nominations and nine Golden Glove Awards. In 2002, TV Guide named *Cheers* the 18th Greatest Show of All Time. He is currently a regular on the HBO sitcom *Curb you Enthusiasm*. He also appears, in a supporting role, on the HBO comedy series, *Bored to Death*.

DAN BLOCKER

Bobby Don Blocker was born on December 10, 1928 in De Kalb in East Texas, the son of Mary and Ora Shack Blocker. His family moved to O'Donnell, located in both Lynn and Dawson counties near Lubbock in west Texas.

He played football at Hardin-Simmons University in 1946. He then attended Texas Military Institute and later graduated from Sul Ross State Teacher's College in Alpine, where he earned a master's degree in the dramatic arts. Dan became a high school English and drama teacher in Sonora, Texas, Carlsbad, New Mexico and California. He reportedly worked as a rodeo performer and as a bouncer in a beer joint while a student. By all accounts he is remembered from his school days for his size of 6 ft 3 in and weight of 300 pounds, and as being good-natured despite his intimidating size. Dan was drafted into the Army and served in the Korean War as a First Sergeant.

In 1957 Dan appeared in a Three Stooges short, "Outer Space Jitters", having portrayed the part of "The Goon". Also in 1957 he appeared in the TV series *The Restless Gun* as a blacksmith and an oafish mute. In 1959, Dan guest-starred in an episode of the television series *The Troubleshooters*. Dan then played the middle son on the long-running NBC television series, *Bonanza*. Dan received partial ownership in a successful chain of Ponderosa/Bonanza Steakhouse restaurants in exchange for serving as their commercial spokesman. Dan Blocker died on May 13, 1972 in Los Angeles, California at the age of 43.

MICHAEL LANDON

Eugene Maurice Orowitz (Michel Landon) was born on October 31, 1936 in Forest Hills, a neighborhood of Queens, New York. His father, Eli Maurice Orowitz, was a Jewish American actor and movie theater manager, and his mother, Peggy O'Neill, was an Irish American Catholic dancer and comedienne. In 1941, when Michael was four years old, the family moved to the Philadelphia suburb of Collingswood, New Jersey, where he attended a Conservative synagogue in Haddon Heights. He later attended Collingswood High School.

In high school, Michael was an excellent javelin thrower, his 193'4" toss in 1954 being the longest throw by a high school athlete in the United States that year. He earned an athletic scholarship to the University of Southern California, but he subsequently tore his shoulder ligaments, ending his javelin career.

He then decided on his surname by choosing it from a phone book. His first starring appearance was on the television program *Telephone Time*. Other parts came in movie roles in *I Was a Teenage Werewolf*, *High School Confidential*, and the notorious *God's Little Acre*, as well as many roles on television. In 1959, at the age of 22, Michael had his first starring TV role as Little Joe Cartwright on *Bonanza*, one of the first TV series to be broadcast in color. The show topped the Nielsen ratings and remained number one for three years. After *Bonanza* he starred as Charles Ingalls in *Little House on the Prairie* and Jonathan Smith in *Highway to Heaven*. He also directed many episodes. His twenty-eight years of full-hour television acting surpasses that of TV legends Lucille Ball and James Arness. Sadly, Michael Landon died on July 1, 1991 in Malibu, California at the age of 54.

PETER FALK

Peter Michael Falk was born on September 16, 1927 in New York City, the son of Michael Peter Falk, owner of a clothing and dry goods store, and his wife, Madeline, an accountant and buyer. His father was Hungarian-Polish and his mother Russian. His right eye was surgically removed at the age of three because of a malignant tumor and he has worn a glass eye for most of his life.

Despite the handicap, Peter participated in team sports, mainly baseball and basketball. He attended Ossining High School in Westchester County, New York, where he was a star athlete and president of his senior class.

After graduating from high school in 1945, he briefly attended Hamilton College in Clinton, New York, and then tried to join the armed services as World War II was drawing to a close. Rejected because of his glass eye, he joined the United States Merchant Marines, and served as a cook and mess boy. After being discharged from the Merchant Marines, he attended the University of Wisconsin. He transferred to the New School for Social Research in New York City where he graduated with a bachelor's degree in literature and political science in 1951. He obtained a master's degree in public administration from Syracuse University in 1953. After graduation he became a management analyst with the Connecticut State Budget Bureau in Hartford. He took up acting and appeared in numerous films and television guest roles, has been nominated for an Academy Award twice, and won the Emmy Award on five occasions and the Golden Globe award once. He is best known for his role as Lieutenant Columbo as everyone's favorite rumpled detective in the television series *"Columbo"* which aired from 1971 to 1978, and for his role as an angel who chose to become human in the German film *Wings of Desire*.

LOU COSTELLO

Louis Francis "Lou" Cristillo was born on March 6, 1906 in Patterson, New Jersey to an Italian father from Calabria, and a mother of French and Irish ancestry.

Lou attended school 15 in Paterson and was considered a gifted athlete. He excelled in basketball and reportedly was once the New Jersey state foul shot champion. He also fought as a boxer under the name "Lou King". He took his professional name from actress Helene Costello. In 1927 Lou went to Hollywood to become an actor – but could only find work as a laborer or extra at MGM and Warner Brothers. His athletic skill brought him occasional work as a stunt man, notably in *The Trail of '98*.

Lou returned to the New York City area in the 1930s and while working in vaudeville, he became acquainted with a talented straight man named Bud Abbot. They finally teamed up in 1936 and signed up with the William Morris Agency, which put them on the radio. In 1938 they received national exposure while appearing on *The Kate Smith Hour*, a popular variety show. They were hugely successful, which ultimately led to their signing with Universal Studios in 1940. Lou and Bud made 36 films between 1940 and 1956, and were among the most popular and highest-paid enter-tainers in the world during World War II. Among their most popular films are *Buck Privates, Hold That Ghost, Who Done It, Pardon My Sarong, The Time of Their Lives, Buck Privates Come Home, Abbot and Costello Meet Franken-stein,* and *Abbot and Costello Meet the Invisible Man.* Abbot and Costello are best remembered for their routine "Who's On First." Lou Costello died on March 3, 1959 in Beverly Hills at the age of 52.

JASON ROBARDS

Jason Nelson Robards, Jr. was born on July 26, 1922 in Chicago, Illinois, the son of Hope Maxine and Jason Robards, Sr, who was among the better-known actors of the early twentieth century. The family moved to New York City when Jason was still a toddler, and then moved to Los Angeles, California, when he was six years old.

The teenaged Jason excelled in athletics, running a 4:18 mile during his junior year at Hollywood High School in Los Angeles. Although his prowess in sports attracted interest from several universities, upon his graduation in 1940, Jason joined the Navy. As a radioman 3rd class in the Navy, Jason joined a heavy cruiser warship, the *USS Northampton* in 1941. On December 7, 1941 he was aboard the *Northampton* in the Pacific Ocean 100 miles at sea. The *Northampton* was later directed into the Guadalcanal campaign in World War II, where she participated in the Battle of the Santa Cruz Islands. During the Battle of Tassafaronga on Guadalcanal on the night of November 30, 1942, the *Northampton* was sunk by two Japanese torpedoes. Jason found himself treading water until near daybreak, when he was rescued by an American destroyer.

After the war Jason decided to get into acting and his career started out slowly. He moved to New York City and found small parts – first in radio and then on the stage. His big break was landing the starring role in an off-Broadway-theatre production of O'Neill's *"The Iceman Cometh"*. He won an Obie Award for his stage performance. He went on to star in stage, film, and television and was a winner of the Tony Award, the Academy Award, and the Emmy Award. Jason Robards played the father, Mr. Halloway, in the movie of Ray Bradbury's *Something Wicked This Way Comes*. He died on December 26, 2000 in Bridgeport, Connecticut at the age of 78.

DOCTOR OZ

Mehmet Cengiez Oz was born in Cleveland, Ohio, to Turkish parents Suna and Mustafa, who had immigrated from Konya, Turkey. Mehmet was educated at Tower Hill School in Wilmington, Delaware.

In high school he was an outstanding athlete and played football, basketball, and baseball. He was captain of the football and baseball teams. He also ran track, wrestled, and participated in other sports.

In 1982 he received his undergraduate degree from Harvard University. In 1986, he obtained a joint MD and MBA degree from the University of Pennsylvania School of Medicine and The Wharton School. He was awarded the Captain's Athletic Award for leadership in college and was Class President followed by President of the Student Body during medical school.

Dr. Oz is Vice-Chair and Professor of Surgery at Columbia University. He directs the Cardiovascular Institute and Complementary Medicine Program at New York-Presbyterian Hospital His research interests include heart replacement surgery, minimally invasive cardiac surgery, and health care policy. He has authored over 400 original publications, book chapters, and medical books and has received several patents. He performs around 250 heart operations annually. Dr. Oz has appeared as a health expert on *The Oprah Winfrey Show* for five seasons. He has appeared on *Good Morning America*, the *Today* show, *Larry King Live*, and *The View*. He currently hosts *The Dr. Oz Show* on television and a talk show on Sirius XM Radio.

BRIAN WILSON

Brian Douglas Wilson was born on June 20, 1942 in Inglewood, California. When Brian was two, the Wilson family moved from Inglewood to nearby Hawthorne, California, a town in the greater Los Angeles urban area. At about age two, Brian heard George Gershwin's "Rhapsody in Blue", which had an enormous emotional impact on him.

By most accounts he was a natural leader. At Hawthorne High School, Brian was on the football team as a quarterback, he played baseball, and he was a cross-country runner in his senior year. However, most of his energy was directed toward music. He sang with various students at school functions and with his family and friends at home. Brian taught his two brothers harmony parts that all three would then practice when they were supposed to be asleep.

Brian enrolled at El Camino Community College in Los Angeles, majoring in psychology, in September 1960. He and his brothers, Carl and Dennis Wilson, along with Mike Love and Al Jardine, first jelled as a music group in the summer of 1961, initially named the Pendletones. Brian and Mike Love together created what would become the first single for the band, "Surfin." Recorded on the small Candix label, the song became a top local hit in Los Angeles and reached number seventy-five on the national Billboard sales charts. Without the band's knowledge or permission, Candix Records changed the band's name to The Beach Boys. The Beach Boys went on to major success and were inducted into the Rock and Roll Hall of Fame. In 2008, *Rolling Stone* magazine published a list of the "100 greatest Singers of All Time", and ranked Brian number 52.

BILLY JOEL

William Martin "Billy" Joel was born on May 9, 1949 in the Bronx, New York and raised in the Levittown section of Hicksville, New York. His father Howard was born in Germany; after the advent of the Nazi regime he emigrated to Switzerland and later to the United States. Billy's mother, Rosalind, was born in England to a Jewish family. His parents divorced in 1960, and his father moved to Vienna, Austria. Joel's father was an accomplished classical pianist and Billy reluctantly began piano lessons at an early age.

As a teenager, Billy took up boxing so that he could defend himself. He boxed successfully on the amateur Golden Gloves circuit for a short time, winning twenty-two bouts, but abandoned the sport shortly after having his nose broken in his twenty-fourth boxing match.

Billy attended Hicksville High School, class of 1967, but did not graduate. Due to playing at a piano bar, he was one English credit short of the graduation requirement.. In 1992, he submitted essays to the school board and was awarded his diploma at Hicksville High's annual graduation ceremony – 25 years later. In the mid-1960s he decided to become a full time musician. Since recording his first hit song, "Piano

Man" in 1973, Billy has become the sixth best-selling recording artist and the third best-selling solo artist in the United States. He had Top 10 hits in the 1970s, 1980s, and 1990s and had 33 Top 40 hits in the United States. He is also a six-time Grammy Award winner, a 23-time Grammy nominee, and has sold over 100 million records worldwide. He was inducted into the Songwriter's Hall of Fame (1992), the Rock and Roll Hall of Fame (1999), and the Long Island Music Hall of Fame (2006).

ERNEST HEMINGWAY

Ernest Miller Hemingway was born on July 21, 1899 in Oak Park, Illinois, a suburb of Chicago. His father Clarence was a physician, and his mother Grace a musician, both well-educated and well-respected in the conservative community of Oak Park.

The family owned a summer home called Windermere on Walloon Lake, near Petoskey, Michigan, where Ernest learned to hunt, fish, and camp in the woods and by the lakes of northern Michigan. His early experiences in nature instilled a passion for outdoor adventure, and living in remote or isolated areas. Ernest attended Oak Park and River Forest High School from 1913 until 1917. He took part in a number of sports – boxing, track and field, water polo, and football.

After leaving high school he went to work for *The Kansas City Star* as a cub reporter. Although he stayed there for only six months, he relied on the *Star*'s style guide as a foundation for his writing. Early in 1918 he joined the Red Cross and signed on to be an ambulance driver in Italy. By June of 1918 he was stationed at the Italian Front. On July 8 he was seriously wounded by mortar fire, having just returned from delivering chocolate and cigarettes to the men the front line.

Despite his wound, he carried an Italian soldier to safety, for which he received the Italian Silver Medal of Bravery.

After the war, he produced most of his work between the mid-1920s and the mid-1950s, and his career peaked in 1954 when he won the Nobel Prize in Literature. Many of his works are classics and he published seven novels, six short story collections, and two non-fiction novels during his lifetime. Ernest Hemingway died on July 2, 1961 in Ketchum, Idaho at the age of 61.

GREGORY PECK

Gregory Peck was born on April 5, 1916 in San Diego, California's seaside community of La Jolla, the son of Bernice Mae and Gregory Pearl Peck, who was a chemist and pharmacist. His parents divorced by the time he was six years old and he spent the next few years being raised by his maternal grandmother. His grandmother died thereafter, and his father again took over his upbringing.

At 14, Gregory attended San Diego High School. Upon graduating, he enrolled briefly at San Diego State Teacher's College, joined the track team, and took his first theatre and public-speaking courses. He stayed there for just one academic year, thereafter entering his college of first choice, the University of California, Berkeley. Since he was 6'3' and very strong, he decided to row on the university crew.

After graduating from Berkeley with a BA degree in English, he headed to New York City to study at the Neighborhood Playhouse. His early career started in 1941 by playing the secretary in George Bernard Shaw's play *"The Doctor's Dilemma*. Because of a back injury he was exempt from the military in World War II. Gregory would go on to be 20th

Century Fox's most popular film stars from the 1940s to the 1660s, starring in such films as *Twelve O'Clock High, Gentleman's Agreement,* and *Roman Holiday,* with Audrey Hepburn. His most notable performance was in the 1962 film *"To Kill a Mockingbird"*, for which he won the Academy Award. President Lyndon Johnson honored him with the Presidential Medal of Freedom in 1969 for his lifetime humanitarian efforts. The American Film Institute named him among the Greatest Male Stars of All Time, ranking No. 12. Gregory Peck died on June 12, 2003 at Torrance , California at the age of 87.

BILLY BOB
THORNTON

Billy Bob Thornton was born on August 4, 1955 in Hot Springs, Arkansas, the son of Virginia, a psychic, and William, a high-school history teacher and basketball coach. He lived in both Alpine and Malvern, Arkansas during his childhood. He was raised a Methodist, in an extended family in a shack that had neither electricity nor plumbing.

He was a high school baseball player, and tried out for the Kansas City Royals, but was let go after an injury.

After a short period laying asphalt for the Arkansas State Transportation Department, he attended Henderson State University, in Arkadelphia, Arkansas, to pursue studies in psychology, but dropped out after two semesters. In the late 1980s Billy Bob settled in Los Angeles to pursue his career as an actor. He initially had a difficult time and worked a variety of jobs to make ends meet. While working as a waiter for an industry event, he served film director and screenwriter Billy Wilder, one of Hollywood's greatest. Wilder advised Billy Bob to consider a career as a screenwriter, advice he took to heart.

His role as the villain in 1992's *"One False Move"*, which he also co-wrote, brought him to the attention of critics. He put Wilder's advice to good use, and went on to write, direct and star in the independent film *"Sling Blade"*, which was released in 1996 and garnered international acclaim. His screenplay earned him an Academy Award for Best Adapted Screenplay, a Writers Guild of America Award, and an Edgar Award, while his performance received Oscar and Screen Actors Guild nominations for Best Actor. He is also a singer-songwriter and has released three albums.

LIAM NEESON

Liam John Neeson was born on June 7, 1952 in Bally-mena, County Antrim, Northern Ireland, the son of Katherine, a cook, and Bernard, a caretaker at the local Catholic boys' primary school. He was raised Roman Catholic. His name, Liam, is Irish for William.

At age nine, Liam began boxing lessons at the All Saints Youth Club, and later became Ulster amateur senior boxing champion. It was at age eleven that he first stepped on stage after his English teacher gave him the lead role in a school play. From then on, he kept acting in school productions and made a decision to become an actor. Liam entered the Queen's University in Belfast in 1971 and his abilities as a talented footballer emerged, which resulted in him being spotted by Bohemian F. C. manager Sean Thomas. Liam traveled to Dublin for a trial with the club, and was featured briefly when he came on as a substitute in a game against Shamrock Rovers. He was not offered a contract at the club and that remained his only performance in professional football.

After leaving the university, he returned to Ballymena and worked a variety of casual jobs. In 1978 he was offered a part in a production at the Project Arts Centre. In 1980, film-maker John Boorman saw him on stage, acting in *Of Mice and Men*, and offered him a part in an upcoming movie, *Excalibur*. Between 1982 and 1987 Liam starred in five films, most notably alongside Mel Gibson and Anthony Hopkins in 1984's *The Bounty* and Robert De Niro and Jeremy Irons in 1986's *The Mission*. His most memorable film is *Schindler's List*. He has been nominated for an Oscar, Golden Globe, and a BAFTA.

AL GORE

Albert Arnold "Al" Gore, Jr. was born on March 31, 1948 in Washington, D. C, to Albert Gore, Sr., a U. S. Representative and Senator from Tennessee, and Pauline, one of the first women to graduate from Vanderbilt University Law School. His paternal ancestors were Scots-Irish who first settled in Virginia in the mid 17th century and moved to Tennessee after the Revolutionary War. He divided his childhood between Washington, D. C. and Carthage, Tennessee.

Al attended St. Alban's School from 1956 to 1965. While at St. Alban's, he played on the varsity football team, threw discus for the track and field team, and participated in basketball, art, and government.

After high school, Al enrolled in Harvard University in 1965, the only college he had applied to. While at Harvard Al became a roommate of Tommy Lee Jones the noted actor, and they became life-long friends.. He graduated with a Bachelor of Arts degree in Government cum laude on June 12, 1969. He then enlisted in the Army in August 1969 and was shipped to Vietnam on January 2, 1971. He was stationed with the 20th Engineer Brigade in Bien Hoa and later received an honorable discharge in May, 1971. He entered

Vanderbilt University Divinity School and later Vanderbilt Law School from 1974 to 1976, however, he did not graduate with a law degree, deciding abruptly in 1976 to run for a seat in the U. S. House of Representatives. He began serving in Congress at the age of 28 and stayed there for the next 17 years. He served as 45th Vice President of the United States from 1993 to 2001 under President Bill Clinton. He is currently an author, business man, and American environmental activist.

BOB DOLE

Robert Joseph "Bob" Dole was born on July 22, 1923 in Russell, Kansas, the son of Bina and Doran Ray Dole. His father, who had moved the family to Russell, Kansas while Bob was still a toddler, had made a living by running a small creamery. During the Great Depression, which hit Kansas very hard, the Dole family moved into the basement of their home and rented out the rest of the house.

Bob graduated from Russell High School in the spring of 1941 and enrolled at the University of Kansas the following fall. Bob, a star high school athlete in his native Russell, earned a spot on the Kansas freshman football team.

In 1942, he joined the Army to fight in World War II. He became a second lieutenant in the Army's 10th Mountain Division. In April 1945, while engaged in combat near Castel d'Aiano in the Apennine mountains southwest of Bologna, Italy, he was hit by German machine gun fire in his upper right back. His right arm was also badly injured. He had to wait nine hours on the battlefield before being taken to the 15th Evacuation Hospital. He began a recovery that would last until 1948 at Percy Jones Army hospital in Battle Creek, Michigan.

Bob ran for office for the first time in 1959 and was elected to the Kansas House of Representatives, serving a two-year term. After graduating from law school at Washburn University in Topeka, he was admitted to the bar and commenced the practice of law in his hometown of Russell in 1952. In 1968, Bob won the Republican nomination for the United States Senate. He was re-elected in 1974, 1980, 1986, and 1992, before resigning on June 11, 1996 to focus on his Presidential campaign in which he was unsuccessful. He is still active in law.

JACK WARDEN

Jack Warden was born on September 18, 1920 in Newark, New Jersey, the son of Laura and John Warden Lebzelter, an engineer and technician. His father was Jewish and his mother was Irish American. He was raised in Louisville, Kentucky.

Jack was expelled from high school for fighting. He eventually fought as a professional boxer under the name Johnny Costello where he had 13 welterweight bouts but earned little money. He worked as a nightclub bouncer, tugboat deckhand and lifeguard before joining the United States Navy in 1938. He was stationed in China for three years with the Yangtze River Patrol. In 1941, he joined the United States Merchant Marines, but, quickly tiring of the long convoy runs, he switched to the United States Army in 1942 where he served as a paratrooper in the 501st Parachute Infantry Regiment, with the elite 101st Airborne Division during World War II. In 1944, on the eve of the D-Day invasion, Staff Sergeant Warden shattered his leg by landing on a fence during a nighttime practice jump in England. After almost a year in the hospital, he recovered enough to participate in the Battle of the Bulge in 1944.

After leaving the military in 1945, he moved to New York City and pursued an acting career on the G. I. Bill. In 1948 he made his television debut on *The Philco Television Playhouse* and *Studio One*. He first film role was in *The Man with My Face* in 1951, and in 1952 he began a three-year role in the television series *Mr. Peepers*. He had a role in *From Here to Eternity* and a breakthrough film role in *12 Angry Men*. He has won an Emmy Award and nominations for Academy Awards for Best Supporting Actor. He has appeared in over one hundred movies.

GEORGE S. PATTON

George Smith Patton, Jr. was born on December 21, 1885 in San Gabriel Township, California to George Smith Patton, Sr. and Ruth Wilson. The Pattons were an affluent family of Scottish descent. His father was an acquaintance of John Singleton Mosby, a noted cavalry leader of the Confederate Army in the Civil War. The younger Patton grew up hearing Mosby's stories of military glory. After high school George attended Virginia Military Institute for one year. He then transferred to the United States Military Academy at West Point. He was appointed Cadet Adjutant (the second highest position for a cadet), eventually graduating in 1909.

George participated in the 1912 Summer Olympics in Stockholm in the first-ever modern pentathlon. He placed sixth out of 37 contestants in 300 meter freestyle swimming. He was third out of 29 fencers. In the equestrian cross-country steeplechase he was among the three riders who turned in perfect performances. He "hit the wall" 50 yards from the finish line of the four kilometer cross-country footrace, and then fainted after crossing the line at a walk. He finished third out of 15 contestants in that event and finished fifth overall in the Olympics.

In 1916-17 he participated in the unsuccessful Pancho Villa Expedition. In World War I, he was the first officer assigned to the new United States Tank Corps and saw action in France. In World War II he commanded corps and armies in North Africa, Sicily, and the European Theater. He was later given command of the Third Army and ably led it in breaking out of the hedgerows of Normandy. George Patton died from the results of an automobile accident in Heidelberg, Germany on December 21, 1945.

NORMAN
SCHWARZKOPF

Norman Schwarzkopf was born on August 22, 1934 in Trenton, New Jersey, the son of Ruth and Herbert Schwarzkopf. His father served in the U. S. Army before becoming the Superintendent of the New Jersey State Police, where he worked as a lead investigator on the infamous Lindbergh kidnapping, but returned to an Army career and rose to the rank of Major General.

Norman, being an Army brat, attended the Community High School in Tehran, later the International School of Geneva and finally he graduated from Valley Forge Military Academy. After high school, Norman entered the United States Military Academy. While at West Point he played on the football team, wrestled, sang and conducted the chapel choir.

He graduated 43rd in his class in 1956 with a Bachelor of Science degree and was commissioned a Second Lieutenant. He became and aide-de-camp to the Berlin Brigade in 1960 and 1961. In 1965, after completing his master degree at the University of Southern California, he served at West point as an instructor in the mechanical engineering department.

He would go on to serve in Vietnam as a task force adviser. During the 1970s, Norman's star continued to rise. He attended the U. S. Army War College at Carlisle Barracks, Pennsylvania, served on the Army General Staff at The Pentagon, was deputy commander of U. S. Forces Alaska, and served a brigade commander at Fort Lewis, Washington. In 1988 he was promoted to General and was appointed Commander-in-Chief of the U. S. Central Command and as such, was commander of the Coalition Forces in the Gulf War of 1991. General Schwarzkopf was also known as "Stormin' Norman" and "The Bear" and is currently retired from the Army.

ED HARRIS

Edward Allen "Ed" Harris was born on November 28, 1950 in Englewood, New Jersey, the son of Margaret, a travel agent, and Robert, who sang with the Fred Waring chorus and worked at the bookstore of the Art Institute of Chicago. He was raised into a middle-class Presbyterian family.

He graduated from Tenafly High School in 1969 where he played on the football team, serving as the team's captain in his senior year. He was a star athlete in high school and competed in athletics at Columbia University in 1969.

Two years later his family moved to New Mexico and he followed after having discovered his interest in acting. He enrolled at the University of Oklahoma to study drama. After several successful roles in the local theater, he moved to Los Angles, California, and enrolled at the California Institute of the Arts. His first important film role was in *Borderline* with Charles Bronson. In *Knightriders* he played the king of a motorcycle-riding renaissance-fair troupe in a role modeled after King Arthur. In 1983 he became a star, playing astronaut John Glenn in *The Right Stuff*. Twelve years later, a film with a similar theme led to Ed being nominated for an Academy Award for Best Supporting Actor for his portrayal of NASA mission director Gene Kranz in *Apollo 13*. Further Oscar nominations arrive in 1999, 2001, and 2003. Along with theatrical films, he has starred in television adaptations of *Riders of the Purple Sage,* and *Empire Falls*. He has been nominated for four Academy Awards, two BAFTA Awards, one Emmy Award, and four Golden Globe Awards (he won in 1998). He is currently an actor, writer, and director.

LAURENCE TUREAUD (MR. T)

Laurence Tureaud was born on May 21, 1952 in Chicago, Illinois, the youngest son in a family with twelve children. His father, Nathaniel Tureaud Sr. was a minister. He grew up in one of the city's housing projects, Robert Taylor Homes.

Laurence attended Dunbar High School, where he played football, wrestled, and studied martial arts. He won a football scholarship to Prairie View A&M University, where he majored in mathematics, but was expelled after his first year. He then enlisted in the U. S. Army and served in the Military Police Corps. After his discharge, he tried out for the Green Bay Packers, but failed to make the team due to a knee injury. He then went to work as a bounder and it was at this time that he created the persona of "Mr. T". He managed eventually to parlay his job as a bounder into a career as a body guard to the stars that lasted almost ten years. He protected well-known personalities like Muhammed Ali, Steve McQueen, Michael Jackson, Leon Spinks, Joe Frazier, and Diana Ross, charging $1,000 per day.

In 1980, Mr. T was spotted by Sylvester Stallone and landed a role in *Rocky III*. He appeared in two more films before accepting a television series role on *The A-Team*, playing Sergeant Bosco "B.A." (Bad Attitude) Bar, an ex-army commando on the run with three other members from the U. S. government "for a crime they didn't commit". His role in *The A-Team* led to him making many other television appearances. In 1984, he made a motivational video called "Be Somebody... or Be Somebody's Fool!" In 2006 he starred in the reality show *I Pity the Fool*, shown on TV Land, the title of which comes from his catchphrase from *Rocky III*.

OMAR BRADLEY

Omar Nelson Bradley was born on February 12, 1893 in rural Randolph County, near Clark, Missouri. They were a poor family and Omar attended country schools where his father was the teacher, however, his father died when Omar was nine. His mother moved to Moberly and remarried.

Omar graduated from Moberly High School in 1911, an outstanding student and captain of both the baseball and football teams. After high school Omar was appointed to the U. S. Military Academy at West Point where he became a football and baseball star. He was considered one of the most outstanding college players in the nation his junior and senior seasons at West point. He lettered in baseball three times, including the 1914 team, from which every player remaining in the army became a general.

He graduated in 1915 and was commissioned into the infantry and was assigned to serve on the U. S. – Mexico border. He joined the 19th Infantry Division in August 1918, which was scheduled for European deployment, but the armistice was signed ending the war. Between the wars, he taught at West Point, and after 1938 he was directly under Army chief of Staff George Marshall. In February 1941, he was promoted to brigadier general. He did not receive a front-line command until early 1943 when he was sent North Africa to be Eisenhower's troubleshooter. Omar moved to London as commander in chief of the American ground forces preparing to invade France in 1944. At D-Day he was chosen to command the U. S. 1st Army. He was the last surviving five-star general and the first Chairman of the Joint Chiefs of Staff. Omar Bradley died on April 8, 1981 in New York and is buried at Arlington National Cemetery.

DR. PHIL

Phillip Calvin McGraw was born on September 1, 1950 in Vinita, Oklahoma, the son of Jerry and Joe McGraw. He grew up in the oilfields of North Texas where his father was an equipment supplier. During Phil's childhood, his family moved so his father could pursue a lifelong dream of becoming a psychologist.

Phil attended Shawnee Mission North High School in Overland Park, Kansas. 1968, he was awarded a football scholarship to the University of Tulsa, where he played middle linebacker under Coach Glenn Dobbs. On November 23 of that year Tulsa lost to the University of Houston 100-6, which caused Coach Dobbs to retire after the season.

Phil transferred to Midwestern State University in Wichita Falls, Texas. He graduated in 1975 from Midwestern with a Bachelor of Arts degree in psychology. He went on to earn a master's degree in experimental psychology in 1976, and a PhD in clinical psychology in 1979 at the University of North Texas. In 1983, Phil and his father joined Thelma Box, a successful Texas businesswoman, in presenting "Pathways" seminars, an experience-based training which allows individuals to achieve and create their own results.

In 1990, Phil joined lawyer Gary Dobbs in co-founding Courtroom Sciences Inc. (CSI), a trial consulting firm. In 1995, Oprah Winfrey hired Phil's CSI firm to prepare her for the Amarillo Texas beef trial. She was so impressed with him for the victory that she invited him to appear on her show. His appearance proved so successful that he began appearing weekly as a "Relationship and Life Strategy Expert" starting in April 1998. On September 2002 he launched his own syndicated daily television show, *Dr. Phil* which is now a smashing success.

BILLY CRYSTAL

William Edward "Billy" Crystal was born on March 14, 1948 in the Doctor's Hospital in Manhattan, the son of Helen, a housewife, and Jack, a record company executive and producer of jazz records, who owned and operated the Commodore Record store. Billy grew up in a Jewish family that he has described as "large" and "loving."

After graduation from Long Beach High School, Billy attended Marshall University in Huntington, West Virginia, on a baseball scholarship, having learned the game from his father, who pitched for St. John's University. He never played a game at Marshall because the program was suspended during his freshman year and he didn't return as a sophomore.

He then went on to Nassau Community College, and later attended New York University where he graduated with a B. F. A. from NYU's Tisch School of the Arts in 1970. He studied film and television direction under Martin Scorsese at NYU. He appeared on an episode of *All in the Family* and was on the dais for the Dean Martin Celebrity Roast of Muhammad Ali on February 19, 1976. He is probably most remembered for his role as Jodi Dallas on the ABC sitcom *Soap* in the 1970s. He did do a stand-up bit on the first season of Saturday Night Live and in 1984 joined the cast. His first film role was in Joan River's 1978 film *Rabbit Test*. He also made game show appearances on *The Hollywood Squares, All Star Secrets,* and *The $20,000 Pyramid*. He starred in several movies such as *When Harry Met Sally, City Slickers, Mr. Saturday Night,* and *Forget Paris*. He has hosted the Academy Awards eight times.

CHARLIE ROSE

Charles Pete "Charlie" Rose, Jr. was born on January 5, 1942 in Henderson, North Carolina, the only child of Margaret and Charles Pete Rose, Sr., tobacco farmers who owned a country store. As a child, Charlie lived above his parent's store in Henderson and helped out with the family business from age seven.

A high school basketball star, he entered Duke University intending to pursue a degree with a pre-med track, but an internship in the office of Democratic North Carolina Senator B. Everett Jordan got him interested in politics.

Charlie graduated in 1964 with a bachelor's degree in history. He earned a Juris Doctor from the Duke University School of Law in 1968, and also attended New York University Stern School of Business. In 1972, while working at Bankers Trust, he landed a job as a weekend reporter for WPIX-TV. His break came in 1974, after Bill Moyers hired him as managing editor for the PBS series *Bill Moyers' International Report*. In 1975, Moyers named him executive producer of *Bill Moyers' Journal* where he began appearing more on camera. "*A Conversation with Jimmy Carter*" won a 1976 Peabody Award. He worked at several networks until

KXAS-TV in Dallas-Fort Worth hired him as program manager and gave him the late-night time slot that would become the *Charlie Rose Show*. Charlie worked for CBS News from 1984 to 1990 as the anchor of CBS News *Nightwatch* which won an Emmy Award in 1987. He was a correspondent for *60 minutes II* from its inception and later a correspondent for *60 Minutes*. In May 2010, he gave the commencement address at North Carolina State University.

GERALDO RIVERA

Geraldo Michael Rivera was born on July 4, 1943 in Brooklyn, New York, the son of Lillian, a waitress, and Cruz "Allen" Rivera, a restaurant worker and cab driver. Geraldo's father was Puerto Rican and his mother was Ashkenazi Jewish, and he was raised mostly Jewish. He grew up in Manhattan and West Babylon, New York. His mother inspired him to become a journalist when she signed him up for a journal camp at his high school in his sophomore year.

After high school he attended the University of Arizona, where he played varsity lacrosse as goalie. From September 1961 to May 1963, he attended the State University of New York Maritime College, where he was a member of the rowing team.

He received his J.D. from Brooklyn Law School in 1969, and did postgraduate work at the University of Pennsylvania that same year. Geraldo was hired by WABC-TV in New York City as a reporter for *Eyewitness News*. In 1972, he garnered national attention and won a Peabody Award for his report on the neglect and abuse of mentally retarded patients at Staten Island's Willowbrook State School and began to appear on ABC national programs such as *20/20* and *Night-*

line. Around this time, Geraldo also began hosting ABC's *Good Night America.* The show featured the famous refrain from Arlo Guthrie's hit "City of New Orleans" as the theme. After Elvis Presley died in 1977, Geraldo then investigated Presley's prescription drug records and concluded that he had died of multiple drug intake. His conclusion caused Tennessee medical authorities to later revoke the medical license of Dr. George C. Nichopoulos, for over prescribing drugs.

DICK CAVETT

Richard Alva "Dick" Cavett was born on November 19, 1936 in Nebraska, but sources differ as to the specific town, locating his birthplace in either Gibbon, where his family lived, or nearby Kearney, the location of the nearest hospital. His mother Erabel and his father Alva both worked as educators. Dick's parents taught in Comstock, Gibbon, and Grand Island, where Dick started kindergarten at Wasmer Elementary School. Three years later, both of his parents landed teaching positions in Lincoln, Nebraska, where Dick completed his education at Capitol, Prescott, and Irving schools and Lincoln High School. When he was ten, his mother, then thirty-six, died of cancer. His father subsequently marred Dorcas Deland, also an educator.

Dick was elected state president of the student council in high school, and was a gold-medalist at the state gymnastics championship. Before leaving for college, he worked as a caddy at the Lincoln Country Club.

He also began doing magic shows for $35 a night and in 1952 he attended the convention of the International Brotherhood of Magicians in St. Louis and won the Best New Performer trophy. Around the same time, he met fellow magician Johnny Carson, eight years his senior, who was dong a magic act at a church in Lincoln. Dick attended Yale University and in his senior year changed his major from English to Drama. After graduating from Yale, he entered the world of television and became a famous talk show host known for his conversational style and in-depth discussion of issues. He appeared regularly on nationally broadcast television in the United States in five consecutive decades, the 1960s through the 2000s. He has won two Emmy Awards, in 1972 and 1974, and has acted in a number of films.

LOU DOBBS

Louis Carl "Lou" Dobbs was born on September 24, 1945 in Childress County, Texas, the son of Frank, a co-owner of a propane business, and Lydia, a bookkeeper. When he was 12, his father's propane business failed and the family moved to Rupert, Idaho.

He attended Minico High School in Minidoka County, where he played tackle on the football team and served as student body president.

Although accepted at the University of Idaho and Idaho State University, he was persuaded to apply to Harvard, where was accepted and later graduated with a Bachelor of Arts degree in economics in 1976. After graduating, Lou worked for federal anti-poverty programs in Boston and Washington, DC. He briefly attended law school at the University of Idaho. He later moved to Yuma, Arizona a got a job as a police and fire reporter for KBLU-AM and by the mid-1970s was a television anchor and reporter in Phoenix. He later joined Seattle's KING-TV. In 1979 he was contacted by a recruiter for Ted Turner for a position at CNN. Lou joined CNN in 1980 serving as its chief economics correspondent and as host of the business news program *Moneyline*. He left

CNN in 1999, rejoined in 2000, and resigned again in 2009. He anchored CNN's *Lou Dobbs Tonight* show until November 2009 when he retired.

Lou describes himself as an "independent populist" and is known for his opposition to NAFTA and support for immigration enforcement. For his reporting, he has won Emmy, Peabody, and Cable ACE awards. He recently gave an interview where he did not rule out the possibility of running for President of the United States in 2012, or he might consider a run for the United States Senate in New Jersey in 2012.

JOHN BELUSHI

John Adam Belushi was born in Chicago, Illinois on January 24, 1949, the son of Agnes, a first generation Albanian-American, and Adam, an Albanian immigrant and restaurant operator who left his native village, Qyteze, in 1934. John grew up outside of Chicago in Wheaton where he attended Wheaton Central High School.

Although John was a little hellion in grade school, he became an all-American boy in high school. He was co-captain of the football team and was elected homecoming king in his senior year.

After high school he began to work as a comedian and got his first big break in 1971, when he joined The Second City comedy troupe in Chicago. He was cast in *"National Lampoon's Lemmings"*, which played Off-Broadway in 1972 and also showcased future SNL performers Chevy Chase and Christopher Guest. From 1973 to 1975, National Lampoon Inc. aired *"The National Lampoon Radio Hour"*, a half-hour comedy program syndicated across the country on approximately 600 stations. John achieved national fame for his work on *"Saturday Night Live"*, which he joined as an original cast member in 1975. Between seasons of the show, he made one of his best-known movies, *"Animal House"*. John left SNL in 1978 to pursue a film career. He would make four more movies; three of them, *"1941"*. *"Neighbors"*, and most notably *"The Blues Brothers"* co-starred fellow SNL alumnus Dan Aykroyd. On John's 30th birthday in 1979, he had the number one film and the number one album in the U.S. Sadly John Belushi died on March 5, 1982 in Los Angeles, California at the age of 33.

DANA CARVEY

Dana Thomas Carvey was born on June 6, 1955 in Missoula, Montana, the son of Billie, a schoolteacher, and William, a high school business teacher. When he was three years old, the family moved to San Carlos, California, in the San Francisco Bay Area.

He attended Tierra Linda Junior High in San Carlos, Carlmont High School in Belmont where he was a member of the champion Cross Country team.

He attended the College of San Mateo and received his Bachelor's degree in communications form San Francisco State University. In 1979, while performing at the Great American Music Hall in San Francisco, he met Paula, who would later become his wife. In his early career he had a minor role in *Halloween II*, and co-starred on *One of the Boys* in 1982, a short-lived television sitcom that also starred Mickey Rooney, Nathan Lane, and Meg Ryan. In 1984, he had a small role in Rob Riener's film *This is Spinal Tap*, in which he played a mime, with fellow comedian Billy Crystal. In 1986, Dana became a household name when he joined the cast of NBC's *Saturday Night Live*. Along with newcomers Phil Hartman, Kevin Nealon, Jan Hooks, and Victoria Jackson, he helped to reverse the show's declining popularity and made SNL "must-see" TV once again. His breakout character was The Church Lady. His other original characters included Garth Algar from "Wayne's World", Hans from "Hans and Franz", and the Grumpy Old Man from "Weekend Update" appearances. He has done many, many impressions of such people as George Bush, Ross Perot, Al Gore, Ted Koppel, Barack Obama, etc. He won an Emmy in 1993 and has a total of six Emmy nominations.

JOHN GOODMAN

John Stephen Goodman was born on June 20, 1952 in Affton, Missouri, the son of Virginia, a store clerk and waitress, and Leslie, a postal worker who died of a heart attack in 1954.

John went to Affton High School where he played football and dabbled in theater. He then won a football scholarship to Southwest Missouri State University. After a college injury ended his football career, he decided to become a professional actor, leaving Missouri for New York in 1975.

He soon found modest success on stage, in commercials and in voice over performances. He was the person who slapped himself in the commercial for Skin Bracer by Mennen, saying the famous line "Thanks...I need that!" He performed off Broadway and in dinner theatres before getting character roles in movies during the early 1980s. In 1982 he landed small movie roles but continued to work on the stage, starring in the Tony-winning Broadway musical *Big River* from 1985 to 1987. For his role of Pap Finn, he received a Drama Desk nomination for Best Featured Actor in a Musical. His most famous role was as Dan Conner on the American sitcom *Roseanne*, which aired on ABC from 1988 to

1997. He had a long history of appearances on late night comedy shows, and was the first guest on *Late Night with Conan O'Brien*, which won him the show's "First Guest Medal". He was a popular guest host on NBC's *Saturday Night Live*, hosting the show thirteen times, while also making seven cameo appearances as Linda Tripp during the Monica Lewinsky scandal. He is noted for his work in numerous films including *Raising Arizona, Barton Fink, The Big Lebowski,* and *O Brother, Where Art Thou.*

DAVID HARTMAN

David Downs Hartman was born on May 19, 1935 in Pawtucket, Rhode Island of German descent.

He attended Mount Hernon School and was gearing toward a professional baseball career in high school. However, he turned down a baseball scholarship to attend Duke University where he majored in economics.

After college, he served three years active duty as an officer in the U. S. Air Force, Strategic Air Command. He was a Supply Officer at Dow AFB in Bangor, Maine and acted in local musicals there, including *Oklahoma*, in the role of Curly. After his military career, he appeared in two Broadway shows, the original *Hello, Dolly* in 1964 and *The Yearling* in 1965. After working in films for awhile, he refocused on television, and won serious attention as a dedicated doctor on *The Bold Ones: The New Doctors*, winning a nomination for a Golden Globe award. He also appeared as the character David Sutton in more than two dozen episodes of the television series *The Virginian*. He starred in the Disney movie *The Island at the Top of the World* in 1974 and a year earlier, did a remake of the holiday classic *Miracle on 34ᵗʰ Street*. In November 1975, David became the first co-host of ABC's new show *Good Morning America*. During his 11 years as host, the show became the highest rated morning news program, and during the show he conducted more than 12,000 interviews. He has been an anchor and host of a series of documentaries on the Discovery Channel and PBS. In North Carolina, David Hartman is also heard on North Carolina Public Radio and WCPE-FM as host of the North Carolina Symphony radio broadcasts.

HUGH LAURIE

James Hugh Calum Laurie was born on June 11, 1959 in Oxford, England His father "Ran" Laurie was a medical doctor who also won an Olympic gold medal in the uncoxed pairs (rowing) at the 1948 London Games. Hugh was raised in the Scottish Presbyterian church, though he has declared "I don't believe in God." He was brought up in Oxford and attended the Dragon School and later Eton. After high school he attended Selwyn College, Cambridge, where he achieved a Third-Class Honours degree in archaeology and anthropology and was a member of the prestigious Hawks' Club.

Like his father, Hugh was an oarsman at school and university. In 1977, he was a member of the junior coxed pair that won the British national title, before representing Britain's Youth Team at the 1977 Junior World Rowing Championships. In 1980, Hugh and his rowing partner, J. S. Palmer, were runners-up in the Silver Goblets coxless pairs for Eton Viking rowing club. Later, he also achieved a Blue while taking part in the 1980 Oxford and Cambridge Boat Race.

Forced to abandon rowing during a bout of infectious mononucleosis, he joined the Cambridge Footlights, which has been the starting point for many successful British co-medians. Hugh formed a comedy team with Emma Thompson and Stephen Fry and they took their annual revue, "The Cellar Tapes," to the Edinburgh Festival Fringe and won the first Perrier Comedy Award. Hugh and Stephen went on to work together on various projects throughout the 1980s and 1990s, including the TV series *The Black Adder*. Hugh also played a role in Emma Thompson's Academy Award winning adaptation of *Sense and Sensibility*. Since 2004, Hugh has starred as Dr. Gregory House on television, for which he has received two Golden Globe Awards and several Emmy nominations.

DAVID ADKINS
(SINBAD)

David Adkins was born on November 10, 1956 in Benton Harbor, Michigan, the son of Martha and the Baptist Rev. Dr Donald Adkins.

He attended Benton Harbor High School, where he was in the marching band as well as the math club. He attended college from 1974 to 1978 at the University of Denver in Denver, Colorado, and he lettered two seasons for the basketball team. He then served in the U. S. Air Force as a boom operator aboard KC-135 Stratotankers. While assigned to the 344th Air Refueling Wing at McConnell Air Force Base in Wichita, Kansas, he would often go downtown to do stand-up comedy, and competed as a comedian/MC in the USAF Talent Contest in 1981. He was almost dismissed with a dishonorable discharge for various misbehaviors, including going AWOL. He said "I didn't make the Air Force basketball team and went into denial, so I kept going AWOL." However, he was eventually discharged honorably from the Air Force.

Under the professional name Sinbad, he began his career appearing on *Star Search*. He won his round against fellow comedian Dennis Miller. His next stint was when he was cast in *The Redd Foxx Show* which was a short-lived sitcom. In

1987, Sinbad landed a role in *A Different World*, a spin-off of *The Cosby Show* for Lisa Bonet's character Denise Huxtable. While Bonet only stayed with the program for a season, Sinbad stayed with the cast from 1988 until 1991 as "Coach Walter Oakes". From 1991 to 1993 he appeared in a few films, videos, and various television shows. By the early 1990s, his popularity had grown enough for Fox to green-light *The Sinbad Show* which premiered in September 1993.

KATHLEEN TURNER

Mary Kathleen Turner was born on June 19, 1954 in Springfield, Missouri, the daughter of Patsy and Allen Turner, a U. S. Foreign Service officer and schoolteacher who grew up in China. Her father, a diplomat, had been imprisoned by the Japanese for four years during the Second World War.

As a child, Kathleen lived in Canada, Venezuela, the United Kingdom and was living in Cuba when Castro came to power. While attending high school in London, she was a gymnast and a very good one. Years later, she played a former gymnast in the movie *War of the Roses*.

Kathleen graduated from the American School in London in 1972 but her father died that same year of a coronary thrombosis and the family moved back to the United States. She attended Southwest Missouri State University at Springfield for two years where she was a classmate of John Goodman. She then earned her Bachelor of Fine Arts degree from the University of Maryland, Baltimore County in 1977.

In 1978, Kathleen made her television debut in the NBC soap *The Doctors*. She made her film debut in 1981 as the ruthless Matty Walker in the thriller *Body Heat*, a role which would bring her to international prominence. *Empire Magazine* cited the film in 1995 when it named her one of the 100 Sexist Stars in Film History. She would ultimately become one of the top box office draws and most sought after actresses in the 1980s and early 1990s. After *Body Heat,* she steered away from femme fatale roles to prevent typecasting. Consequently, her first project after this was the 1983 comedy *The Man with Two Brains.* She starred in *Romancing the Stone* with Michael Douglas, which was a surprise hit and for which she won a Golden Globe Award.

WARREN BEATTY

Warren Beatty was born on March 30, 1937 in Richmond, Virginia. His mother Kathlyn was a Nova Scotia born drama teacher, and his father Ira was a professor of psychology, a public school administrator, and a real estate agent. The family was Baptist. His father moved the family from Richmond to Norfolk, Virginia, and then to Arlington, Virginia, where he became a middle school principal. The family also lived in Waverly, Virginia in the 1930s.

Warren was a star football player at Washington-Lee High School in Arlington. Encouraged to act by the success of his sister (Shirley MacLaine), who had recently established herself as a Hollywood star, he decide to work as a stagehand at the National Theater in Washington, D. C. Upon graduation from high school, he turned down a football scholarship to enroll in drama school. Years later, when he wrote, starred in, and directed *Heaven Can Wait* (a remake of *Here Comes Mr. Jordan*), he made the hero a football player instead of a boxer, and did his own stunts.

He studied acting and directing the Northwestern University School of Drama. He dropped out of Northwestern after his freshman year to enroll in the Stella Adler Conservatory of Acting in New York City. By the age of twenty-two, Warren had appeared in about forty Off Broadway productions. He garnered a best actor Tony Awards nomination in 1960 for his performance in *A Loss Of Roses*. He started his career making appearances in television series such as *Studio One, Playhouse 90,* and *The Many Loves of Dobie Gillis*. He made his film debut opposite Natalie Wood in *Splendor in the Grass*, a box office success for which he was nominated for a Golden Glove Award. At age 30 he achieved critical acclaim and power as a producer and star of *Bonnie and Clyde* which was nominated for 10 Academy Awards. He is presently a producer, director, screenwriter, and actor.

ROY ACUFF

Roy Claxton Acuff was born on September 15, 1903 in Maynardville, Tennessee to Ida Carr and Simon Acuff. The Acuffs were a fairly prominent Union County family. Roy's paternal grandfather had been a Tennessee state senator, and his maternal grandfather was a local physician. Roy's father was an accomplished fiddler and a Baptist preacher, and his mother was proficient on the piano. The Acuff family relocated to Fountain City, a suburb of North Knoxville, in 1919.

Roy attended Central High School, where he had a passion for athletics. He was a three-sport standout at Central, and after graduating in 1925, he was offered a scholarship to Carson-Newman, but turned it down. He played with several small baseball clubs around Knoxville, working at odd jobs, and occasionally boxed. In 1929 he tried out for the Knoxville Smokies, at that time a minor league baseball team for the New York Giants. A series of collapses in spring training following a sunstroke, however, ended his baseball career prematurely. The effects left him ill for several years, and he even suffered a nervous breakdown in 1930.

In 1932, Dr. Hauer's medicine show hired Roy as one of its entertainers and Roy learned to sing loud enough to be heard above the din, a skill that would later help him stand out in early radio. He would later gain regional fame as the singer and fiddler for his group, the Smokey Mountain Boys. He joined the Grand Ole Opry in 1938 and he remained one of the Opry's key figures and promoters for nearly four decades. In 1942, he co-founded the first major Nashville-based country music publishing company. He would go on to become the first living person to be inducted into the Country Music Hall of Fame.

LIONEL RICHIE

Lionel Brockman Richie was born on June 20, 1949 in Tuskegee, Alabama. He grew up on the campus of Tuskegee Institute, as his grandfather's house was across the street from the home of the president of the Institute. His family moved to Illinois where he graduated from Joliet Township High School, East Campus.

A star tennis player in Joliet, he accepted a tennis scholarship at Tuskegee Institute and later graduated with a major in economics.

After receiving his undergraduate degree from Tuskegee, he briefly attended graduate school at Auburn University. In 1968 he became a singer and saxophonist with The Commodores. They signed a recording contract with Atlantic Records in 1968 for one record before moving on to Motown Records, initially as a support act to The Jackson 5. The Commodores then became established as a popular soul group. Their first several albums had a danceable, funky sound. Over time, Lionel wrote and sang more romantic, easy-listening ballads. By the late 1970s, he had begun to accept songwriting commissions from other artists. He composed "Lady" for Kenny Rogers, which hit No. 1 in 1980, and produced Roger's album *Share Your Love* the following year. Lionel and Kenny maintained a strong friendship in later years. In 1981, Lionel sang the theme song for the film *Endless Love*, a duet with Diana Ross. Issued as a single, the song topped the UK and U. S. pop music charts, and became one of Motown's biggest hits. He would go on to have a tremendously successful career and is one of the most admired entertainers of our generation He is still an active singer-songwriter and record producer who has sold more than 100 million records.

ABOUT THE AUTHOR

E.W. SMITH, JR.

Elige Wilson Smith, Jr. was born on February 20, 1933 in Piave, Mississippi, a small rural community in southeast Mississippi. His father was initially a farmer but during the depression landed a job as an automobile mechanic making $8.00 per week. When World War II broke out, the family moved to Mobile, Alabama when the elder Smith got a job at a local Air Force Base.

E. W., Jr. grew up in Mobile and graduated from Murphy High School in 1951. He then entered the Navy in 1952 and served as an aviation electronics technician at a Navy base in Sanford, Florida. After his discharge in 1954, E. W., Jr. entered college at Mississippi Southern and later the University of Alabama on the G.I. Bill. He transferred to Georgia Tech and graduated from there in 1960 with a Bachelor's Degree in Electrical Engineering. After graduation he held several jobs with several companies as an electrical design engineer and worked on such diverse projects as B-52 radar systems, Army Pershing Missile, Army electromagnetic test range, NASA's "Surveyor" moon probe, and Federal Water Pollution research. He joined the Federal Government's Indian Health Service in 1975 and served as the Director of Management

Information Systems.   He later would return to private industry and was a Marketing Director for the Ford Aerospace
Company.

He retired in 1996 and currently lives in Germantown,
Maryland just outside of Washington, D. C. He is the author
of *Dieter's Checklist*, published by Doubleday in 1975, and
Spanish, Mexican, and Early American Ruins of Arizona, a
manuscript unpublished, and *Athletes Once: 100 Famous
People with Sports Backgrounds* (Fireship Press).

Six Who Dared: The Lives of Six Great Soldiers of Fortune
by
Richard Harding Davis

Six Who Dared outlines the lives of six of the most daring, most outrageous, most endearing soldiers of fortune in history.

- **William Walker:** If comfortable careers in law, medicine and the church bore you, perhaps you should consider invading various countries with a handful of men until you can eventually become president of one?
- **Ronald Douglas:** Born into wealth, married into even more, Douglas died broke—and as a hero in eighteen countries.
- **James Hardin-Hickey:** When you come across an uninhabited island in the Atlantic, why not declare it a kingdom and yourself as it's king—at least until England decides she wants the place.
- **Winston Churchill:** What better way for a young man to see action than to become a war correspondent, serve in numerous campaigns, get captured, and stage one of the most daring escapes in history?
- **Philo McGiffin:** When you graduate near the bottom of your class at the U.S. Naval Academy and your own country won't even give you a commission, what else is there to do but command a squadron of Chinese battleships and become commandant of their naval academy?
- **Frederick Burnham:** Just your basic story of how a city boy from Pasadena, CA grows up to be the the finest scout in Africa, and have more hair-raising adventures than Indiana Jones.

"A powerful and original writer." - Theodore Roosevelt

**For the Finest in
Nautical and Historical
Fiction and Nonfiction
*www.FireshipPress.com***

Interesting • Informative • Authoritative

CPSIA information can be obtained at www.ICGtesting.com
ed in the USA
2244090815
V00023B/241/P